PERSPECTIVE FROM PATMOS
The Mind of the Revelator

To Donna From [signature]

Prov 3:5,7

Perspective from PATMOS

THE MIND OF THE REVELATOR

C. M. STEVENS

Guardian BOOKS

Belleville, Ontario, Canada

PERSPECTIVE FROM PATMOS
Copyright © 2006, Clare M. Stevens

All Scripture quotations, unless otherwise specified, are from *The Holy Bible, New International Version.* Copyright © 1973, 1978, 1984 International Bible Society. Used by permission of Zondervan Publishing House. All rights reserved.

Scripture quotations marked NKJV are taken from the New King James Version. Copyright © 1979, 1980, 1982. Thomas Nelson Inc., Publishers.

Scripture quotations marked KJV are taken from *The Holy Bible, King James Version.* Copyright © 1977, 1984, Thomas Nelson Inc., Publishers.

Library and Archives Canada Cataloguing in Publication
Stevens, Clare M., 1944-
Perspective from Patmos : the mind of the revelator / Clare M.Stevens.
ISBN 1-55452-094-0

    1. Bible. N.T. Revelation--Commentaries. I. Title.
BS2825.53.S74 2006   228'.07   C2006-904844-4

For more information, please contact:
Clare Stevens
6840 Rockford Place
Delta, BC   V4E 2S5

Guardian Books is an imprint of *Essence Publishing,* a Christian Book Publisher dedicated to furthering the work of Christ through the written word. For more information, contact:
20 Hanna Court, Belleville, Ontario, Canada K8P 5J2.
Phone: 1-800-238-6376 • Fax: (613) 962-3055.
Email: publishing@essencegroup.com
Website: www.essencegroup.com/publishing

*To my wife, June, whose love and
prayers immeasurably bless my life!*

Table of Contents

Preface

T. S. Eliot once said experience and impressions combine in peculiar ways.[1] Since my teens I've been impressed by the power of John's apocalyptic visions, but experience in biblical studies came later, in university, where I was formally exposed to scriptural exegesis and taught the importance of historical meanings. In the years since then, I've studied John's seven visions with particular attention to the concepts, traditions and symbols that shaped them.

Very few of those symbols originate in John's letter. Like all New Testament authors but one, he was born, raised and formally educated as a Jew, and the apocalyptic themes and symbols that fill his visions are rooted in Jewish worship and tradition. To understand John, one must understand his roots. To understand his visions, one must know the meaning he saw in the symbols that define them.

Many popular books on Revelation ignore John's origins, mistake him for a soothsayer and make his visions a chronology of events at the end of history—

which they invariably assume is at hand. With enthusiasm for sensationalism matched only by disdain for scholarly exegesis, they superimpose interpretations taken from thin air on John's symbols and speculate wildly about the future. Recklessly labeling every trend in society as a sign of the "end times," they cite newspaper clippings and media reports, however inconsequential, as certain proof of the Lord's imminent return. That approach to Revelation begins with the false assumption that John is calling us to be seers rather than saints and invariably ends in failed predictions, like the Y2K episode. For centuries, its only contribution has been a similarly embarrassing legacy of wrong guesses.

Another approach lumps John with Israel's prophets and crafts eschatology by seizing proof texts out of context. Like the prophets, John spoke for God in critical times, but he wasn't one of them. From Elijah to Daniel, they lived more than five centuries before him. As a nation's conscience, they saw the cost of disobedience and warned unfaithful people to return to a faithful God. Their warnings failed, and Israel was overrun by Assyria and subsequently enslaved by Babylon. During captivity, the later prophets foresaw its restoration and the rebuilding of its temple. Their prophecies were fulfilled between the testaments. John writes from a New Testament perspective and, more particularly, with the perspective of one being persecuted for his faith.

Experience and impressions prompted me to write a book that captured his thinking as an early Jewish Christian. Living in hopeless exile, he must

have asked fundamental questions about life; but
the worst times, entrusted to God's hands, can
become the best. In the midst of a severe test, John
saw beyond the chaos of his circumstances to the
character of God. As a Jew, he'd been very well educated in Old Testament Scriptures. As a Christian,
he knew Jesus was the fulfillment anticipated in
them. Truths from Israel's past had meaning in the
life of the new Israel—the Church—and John saw a
tapestry of images rooted in Old Testament themes
but revealing the spiritual dynamics that shape
human destiny in every age. At its center he saw the
Redeemer who is truth itself, and that glimpse put
his world in perspective. John's thinking was shaped
by the traditions of Israel, but his faith was energized by the experience of Patmos.

Like him, we travel through uncertainty not
knowing what a day will bring forth, but the spiritual
dynamics governing his world also govern ours. God
still uses its tribulations to purify our perspective
and sanctify our purposes, but the truth He reveals
rarely leads us on a journey to unknown realms.
Most often, it brings perspective to the realms we
know and equips us to face them with truer insight
and wiser priorities.

To equip John, our Lord revealed Himself! In a
time of holy worship, John turned from preoccupa-
tion with circumstances and saw the Redeemer,
whose supremacy is life's ultimate reality and whose
presence exchanges mystery for meaning. To grasp
the real meaning of John's visions, we too must see
beyond circumstances and events to Jesus Christ. A

fresh revelation of Him is infinitely more valuable than perspective on tomorrow. It brings perspective to today! All the treasures of wisdom and knowledge reside in Him—and He already has all of our tomorrows in perspective.

C. S.

Chapter 1

Recovering John's Perspective

To Him who loves us and has freed us from our sins by His blood, and has made us to be a kingdom and priests to serve His God and Father – to Him be glory and power forever and ever. Amen! (Rev. 1:6).

History's uncertain tides ebb and flow over periods of calm and upheaval, and the closing decades of the first century were extremely turbulent. Rome decimated Israel in AD 70, besieging Jerusalem into starvation, seizing it, razing its buildings—including its temple—and slaughtering its citizens in a primitive example of ethnic cleansing. When the carnage ended, Israel was a field of putrefying corpses with few survivors to bury them.

A world view perished with Jerusalem. Jews believed God's purposes for man rested solely in Israel and made no distinction between national identity and spiritual identity. They saw creation as a series of concentric circles. Earth lay at the center of the universe. Israel was the center of the earth. Jerusalem was the center of Israel! The temple was the center of Jerusalem, and the Holy of Holies—God's dwelling place on earth—was at the center of the temple.

For Jews, the temple's destruction was the ultimate horror of the holocaust that brought Israel's history to a close. Much more than a treasured, national landmark, it was built by divine decree as the earthly manifestation of the heavenly court, and early reverence for it has no parallel in modern times. How could God's earthly dwelling fall? How could a nation and culture whose existence embodied His promises vanish?

The early Christian Church put the trauma of Israel's demise in perspective. It knew Israel was only a channel through which the world's redemption would come. Jesus was the appointed Redeemer! His death and resurrection initiated a new covenant, expanding the horizons of God's self-revelation beyond Israel to all mankind. An earthly Israel vanished, but a spiritual Israel took its place. An old order based on geography and race passed away, and a new one defined by faith arose. The Church was now God's chosen people, but its position was tenuous in a world governed by pagan Rome. Having shattered Judaism's foundations, Rome turned its wrath on Christians and washed its dungeons and coliseums with their blood.

During those horrific times, it exiled an early Jewish Christian named John to the remote island of Patmos. This forgotten prisoner was a master of Old

Testament Scripture and history. Israel's fall molded his thinking, and Rome's persecution tried it in the fire. He knew earth was an arena where righteousness and evil did battle, and their conflict was more than a philosophical debate. Imprisonment gave him a front-row view of the world's hatred for the gospel, but it also strengthened his faith. In the face of adversity, John worshiped, and God gave him seven visions that put life in perspective.

With compelling clarity, he saw two spiritual kingdoms in conflict—the Church and the world. The Church was redeemed and destined for joy! The world was rebellious and doomed for judgment. The Church was a holy city born from above, and its citizens stood before God's throne in spotless white as an overcoming multitude (Rev. 7:9). The blood of martyrdom could not soil their robes or mar their purity (Rev. 7:15). They stood with a Lamb on Mt. Zion (Rev. 14:1), waiting patiently for the full revelation of His glory and the day they'd fill heaven's courts with everlasting praise.

The world was an unrighteous Babylon, intoxicating kings and paupers with fleshly enticements. It denied God, left truth dead in the street, reduced morals to convenience, put the godly in graves and the ungodly on thrones. Hideous beasts and dragons cursed it with deceitful tyranny, and the righteous suffered its inevitable rebuke and endured its hatred. John knew it was doomed and saw angels of death and angels of light unleash turmoil and destruction. Horsemen and plagues wreaked havoc while harlots and kings wept and wailed.

John saw these two kingdoms through images belonging to the Jewish culture, worship and Scriptures he'd known from birth. His visions include 278 references to the Torah, but true revelation brings truth to light, and John saw new meaning in its passages. Beginning with Passover, he saw a loose parallel between Israel's history and the Church. Israel was born in Egypt when a lamb's blood spared its sons. The Church was born when a perfect Lamb was sacrificed for the world's sins, and John saw that Lamb enthroned in heaven. God sent physical plagues on Egypt to call Pharaoh to repentance (Exod. 7-11). John saw the trials of a fallen world as plagues calling all humanity to repent (Rev. 9:20;16:9). After crossing the Red Sea, the Israelites sang the "Song of Moses" (Exod. 15:1-19). John saw redeemed multitudes "from every nation, tribe, people and language" (Rev. 7:9) singing the "the song of Moses the servant of God and the song of the Lamb" (Rev. 15:3). God providentially sustained Israel in the wilderness. John saw the Church as a woman sustained by God in the wilderness (Rev. 12:6). In later history, Israel's major foe was the idolatrous empire of Babylon. John saw the kingdom of the flesh as a harlot called Babylon (Rev. 14:8). Israel's heart was Jerusalem. John saw the Church as a new Jerusalem (Rev. 21:2).

John also saw new meaning in the intricacies of worship and liturgy in Israel's temple. Just as temple trumpets once called people in Jerusalem to repentance, he knew heavenly trumpets were sounding calls to repentance in a world everlastingly at odds with the cross (Rev. 8-9). In the temple, smoke from bowls of incense symbolized the prayers of the people. Christian prayers were rising like smoke to heaven's throne (Rev. 8:3-4). John's references to temple liturgy, vestments, lampstands, trumpets, bowls of incense, a scroll, books of life, altars, thrones, crystal seas, elders and living beings so exceed that of other New Testament authors that many commentators believe he was a temple priest prior to his Christian conversion. Alfred Edersheim, an authority on the temple, made this observation:

> John writes, not like an ordinary Israelite. He has eyes and ears for details which others would have left unnoticed...Indeed, the apocalypse, as a whole, may be likened to the Temple services in its mingling of prophetic symbols with worship and praise. But it is specially remarkable, that the temple references with which the Book of Revelation abounds are generally to minutiae, which a writer who had not been familiar with such details...would scarcely have even noticed.[2]

Who, then, is John, and what is this exiled priest saying? Like earlier New Testament authors, he knows man's ultimate destiny is determined by the blood of a victorious Lamb enthroned on high and a coming judgment on sin. Unlike them, he writes after Jerusalem's fall and pays no heed to issues like the relationship between Jew and Gentile, the equality of all believers or the theological implications of law and faith. Instead, he sees faith harshly tested by the new reality of an increasingly hostile pagan world and uses apocalyptic themes to describe the conflict.

John's visions aren't a macabre prediction of doomsdays destined to occur thousands of years after him. Writing to anchor believers in hostile times, he doesn't reveal a world they'll never live to see but the one they know, explaining it with familiar symbols derived mainly from the Old Testament Scriptures. He isn't discerning events on some remote horizon but discerning truth in a pagan world opposed to it, and his symbols put its challenges to faith in perspective.

They also put our world in perspective. Faith is dynamic and lives in the present, but truth's horizons are infinite. The world is still a perpetual battle-ground, where good and evil vie for the affections of the soul and two spiritual kingdoms are locked in conflict, but John's letter isn't a trek into chaos and calamity. His hope is fixed in the Redeemer who is forever unchanging and forever holy. Contrary to popular misconception, John isn't focused on the end of time but on the Master of time. To understand John's perspective is to see our Lord high and lifted up.

With majesty that far outweighs their mystery, John's seven visions penetrate the boundaries of time and history to reveal the Ruler of both and consummate Scripture's witness to the One who was and is and is to come. He's a mighty Warrior who brings all things to account, a great High Priest who counsels His people, a sacrificial Lamb whose blood washes our robes and a righteous Judge who calls us to holiness, faith, patience and endurance. Alive forevermore, creation is under His control and history is subject to His measure! His power is the undeniable constant of human existence, and His triumph is life's all-encompassing certainty. The conflict between two spiritual kingdoms never challenges His sovereignty, and His faithfulness is the assurance weeping will not endure beyond a night. He has the welcoming face of a compassionate Savior who sustains us in the wilderness, and His nature proves one sublime truth—redeeming love is time's crowning glory and eternity's final Word!

Chapter 2

John's First Vision—
Compassionate Counselor

*And when I turned I saw seven golden lampstands,
and among the lampstands was someone "like a son
of man," dressed in a robe reaching down to his feet
and with a golden sash around his chest. His head
and hair were white like wool, as white as snow, and
his eyes were like blazing fire* (Rev. 1:12-14).

Recommended Reading:
Chapters 1 to 3 of Revelation

John is *"in the Spirit"* *"on the Lord's Day"* and
hears a loud voice (Rev. 1:10). Turning, he sees
seven golden lampstands and one *"like a son of
man"* clothed in brilliant priestly garments standing
among them. His holiness shines more brightly than
the sun and He holds *"seven stars"* (Rev. 1:16). A new
covenant means a new high priest, and the vision
implicitly echoes the events of Sinai where God insti-
tuted the old covenant of law (Exod. 31:18). At Sinai,
fire burned on the mountain peak (Exod. 19:18).
Jesus' eyes blaze like fire (Rev. 1:14), exposing the
innermost parts of the soul. At Sinai, God's presence
inspired awe and His voice thundered (Exod. 20:18).
Jesus' voice, like the sound of many waters (Rev.
1:15), thunders also. He has the keys to death and

hell (Rev. 1:18), and His words, like a sharp two-edged sword (Rev. 1:16), lay bare the secrets of the heart.

Apocalyptic symbols don't communicate at the surface. They reveal truths and principles. White, priestly robes, lampstands and seven stars convey truths adapted from Jewish worship and fulfilled in the person of Jesus—our great high priest. Priests wore eight different garments for the varied liturgies of the temple. The simplest was worn in the Holy of Holies during the sacrifices on the Day of Atonement. The most resplendent was worn when the sacrifice was accepted. These sacred vestments were made according to divine instruction, as recorded in the twenty-eighth chapter of Exodus and priests handed them down meticulously to their successors.

John notes Jesus' white robe.[3] White signifies atonement. Israel's temple sacrifices offered for sin required a scapegoat to symbolically carry away the punishment of the people. The high priest tied a cord of red painted wool between its horns and another to the neck of a goat reserved for a sin offering. The cord on the scapegoat was later divided, one-half on its horns and the other at the opening of the sanctuary.[4] When God accepted the sacrifice, both halves turned white. Israel's sacrifices foreshadowed a perfect sacrifice needing no repetition. In John's vision, white symbolizes God's acceptance of Jesus' perfect sacrifice on Calvary. Jesus also wears a gold sash (Rev. 1:13). Since priests wore them only when actively administering temple rites (Exodus 28), Jesus is actively ministering as He walks among the lampstands.

Some translations refer to "seven stars" in His

right hand (Rev. 1:16). Early Jews sometimes spoke of stars as ministering spirits of God. *Seven* indicates completeness. Isaiah foresaw the seven spirits of Jesus' character: *"The Spirit of the LORD will rest on him—the Spirit of wisdom and of understanding, the Spirit of counsel and of power, the Spirit of knowledge and of the fear of the LORD"* (Isa. 11:2).

John's image of Jesus as high priest robed in white and gold holding seven stars is a composite portrait of three perfections. In white, He is the perfect sacrifice for sin. In gold, He perfectly intercedes for us. Bearing seven stars, He incorporates all the perfection of divinity in His being.

John sees Jesus among menorah lampstands—sacred fixtures that stood in the temple to represent the light of God's Word. Like priestly garments, the menorah was made under divine instruction as recorded in Exodus:

> *"Make a lampstand of pure gold and hammer it out, base and shaft; its flowerlike cups, buds and blossoms shall be of one piece with it. Six branches are to extend from the sides of the lampstand—three on one side and three on the other...Then make its seven lamps and set them up on it so that they light the space in front of it. Its wick trimmers and trays are to be of pure gold...See that you make them according to the pattern shown you on the mountain"* (Exod. 25:31,32,37,38,40).

The menorah still appears on Israel's state emblem, often pictured with a Torah scroll because light and truth are related. The psalmist said; "*The entrance of thy words giveth light*" (KJV) and called the Word "*a lamp unto my feet*" (KJV). Zechariah linked the light of the menorah and the olive oil used for anointing with the Spirit of God.

> *He asked me, "What do you see?" I answered, "I see a solid gold lampstand with a bowl at the top and seven lights on it, with seven channels to the lights. Also there are two olive trees by it, one on the right of the bowl and the other on its left"...So he said to me, "...'Not by might nor by power, but by my Spirit,' says the LORD Almighty*" (Zech. 4:2,3,6).

John makes the menorah a symbol of the Church, and the parallel is striking. Only high priests could light the menorah, and only Jesus, our Great High Priest, can make us members of His Church through a saving encounter. The menorah symbolized the light of God's Word. The Church proclaims the Word now. Menorah lamps were filled with burning oil. The Church burns with the oil of the Holy Spirit. Menorah lamps had to burn constantly. The Church's light must shine constantly. The menorah had to be pure gold. God's standard for His Church is purity.

Seven Churches

> "*Write therefore, what you have seen, what is now and what will take place later. The mystery of the seven stars you saw in my right*

*hand and of the seven golden lampstands is
this: The seven stars are the angels of the
seven churches, and the seven lampstands are
the seven churches"* (Rev. 1:19-20).

In a voice thundering like many waters, our Lord
tells John to write Ephesus, Smyrna, Pergamum,
Thyatira, Sardis, Philadelphia and Laodicea. These
cities were important hubs, and a circular letter to
them would reach all Christians in Asia Minor, but
addressing their seven churches may be more than
an accident of geography. In temple worship, seven
was the number of the covenant. In apocalyptic
style, it signified completeness. The problems these
churches face typify all Christendom under the new
covenant in every age.

Some make an allegory of the seven churches,
claiming they represent seven distinct ages of Church
history. Ephesus, the church that left its first love, is
always labeled as the early Church. Lukewarm
Laodicea is always the Church today. Allegorists selectively revise the rest of history into five more ages to
complete their model, but it presents two problems.

First, generalizing isn't accurate. For example, first
century churches like Smyrna and Philadelphia had
not lost their first love and can't be lumped with
Ephesus. Similarly, many members of churches in the
Third World today suffer martyrdom under oppressive
regimes, yet the churches are alive and vibrant. They
can't be called lukewarm and lumped with Laodicea.

The second issue is even more difficult. If John's
letter was an allegory of Church ages, history was

predetermined when he wrote it. If so, why write? Calling the Church to repent of predetermined failures would be senseless.

More correctly, John writes to encourage believers to consecration and faithfulness—not to preview Church history. Our Lord's counsel is highly personal and manifests the seven spirits described by Isaiah—referred to in some translations as "seven stars." With perfect insight, He can say to each church, "I know thy works!"

Ephesus—Love

> *"You have persevered and have endured hardships for my name, and have not grown weary. Yet I hold this against you: You have forsaken your first love"* (Rev. 2:3-4).

Beginning at Ephesus, our Lord praises its toil, labor, doctrinal purity and endurance under persecution. But, in very sad words, He says it has left its first love. In Greek, *left* means "departed, forsaken or left behind." Doctrine defines faith, but love energizes it! What value has sound doctrine if love has waned? In this passage, the loving spirit of the Lord who rightly claims ownership is reaching out to Ephesians, only to sense their indifference. Loving hearts feel the pain of rejection most keenly.

The soul was made for love and instinctively seeks it. The newly converted invariably sense they've found the missing meaning of life and experience new freedom and emotional fulfillment in love for God.

Faith works by love, and those who come to it find new love for prayer, the Scriptures and the fellowship of the Church. However, first love is not simply a yardstick measuring a new convert's enthusiasm. Our Lord demands first place in our lives, and that truly defines "*first love.*"

Unattended, love's fire dims and self-indulgence takes precedence. The true object and source of love is God, and the soul can't thrive on substitutes. To renew one's first love, lesser loves must be dethroned—and that requires repentance! In extremely serious words, Jesus warns Ephesus to repent or He will remove its lampstand (Rev. 2:5). His language recalls history. In the era between the Old and New Testament, Jerusalem was invaded. The temple was desecrated and its lamp extinguished. A temple without the light of the menorah was a sacrilege. Religion without the light of holy love is also.

Smyrna—Wisdom

> "*I know your afflictions and your poverty —yet you are rich!*" (Rev. 2:9).

Smyrna faces adversity as some Christians pay for their faith with the loss of livelihood and possessions. Our Lord knows their "*afflictions and...poverty.*" No stranger to persecution and suffering, He endured the cross for the joy set before Him (Heb. 12:2) and commends Smyrna without qualification for its faithfulness under fire.

Faithlessness can't cope with adversity. Atheists often claim evil proves there's no God, but their claim offers neither logic nor hope. In a godless universe, life is just the result of an accident in space and man is only matter. Good and evil don't exist, and death is of no more consequence than the evaporation of a bucket of water. Why call anything evil? *Unappealing,* perhaps! Why *evil?* Good and evil can only be defined if souls are made in the image of a holy Creator with value beyond matter. The atheist who denies God forfeits his right to speak of evil. More tragically, he forfeits hope as well, since he's left with nothing but futility.

Faith that's weak also fails in adversity. It stumbles over life's reverses and rewrites its theology out of quiet anger towards God. This world isn't final! An hour has already been appointed when it will pass away! Why reap a harvest of joyless living clinging stubbornly to trifles rather than to God's hand? Life's refining fires always yield both gold and dross. The wise keep the gold and discard the dross. Fools keep the dross and discard the gold. Smyrna makes the wise choice—trust! Tempered by refining fire, it shines as gold. With the spirit of wisdom, our Lord commends it and encourages the Christians there to "*Be faithful until death, and I will give you the crown of life*" (NKJV).

Pergamum—Understanding

> "*Nevertheless, I have a few things against you: You have people there who hold to the teaching of Balaam*" (Rev. 2:14).

Pergamum, center of pagan worship, is affluent and decadent, and our Lord calls it "*where Satan has his throne*" (Rev. 2:13). It celebrates every vice and persecutes Christians, including a martyr named Antipas reputedly baked in a brass container for refusing to deny the Lord.[5] Even so, the church perseveres. Like in Pergamum, rotting western culture seeks to expel every vestige of Christian influence and increasingly resembles a satanic throne room where millions of aborted corpses lie putrefying and where lives and homes broken by drugs or divorce strew the floor while demonic choirs exalt degradation.

When Satan can't destroy churches from without, he tries from within and often uses the permissiveness of secular culture to desensitize believers to the holiness of their calling. Jesus warns Pergamum of two dangerous heresies—the teachings of Balaam and of the Nicolaitans. Balaam, mentioned in Numbers 22 to 24, led Israel to compromise with sensual, idolatrous cults. The Nicolaitans were a libertine sect that taught that freedom in Christ meant freedom to sin.[6] Irenaeus said they lived in "unrestrained indulgence." Our Lord says "*the practices of the Nicolaitans...I also hate*" (Rev. 2:6).

Those who see grace as a license to sin usually see God as a schizophrenic torn between indulgent love and judgmental holiness, and they reduce the atonement to an attempt to reconcile the two. This is mistaken. God is perfect! His holiness is perfect in love, and His love is perfect in holiness. In perfect harmony, both attributes announced to the world, "*Thou shalt call his name JESUS: for he shall save his people from their sins*" (KJV). Jesus didn't die to reconcile competing attributes of divinity but to reconcile sinners to God, who seeks to "*purify for Himself His own special people, zealous for good works*" (Titus 2:14, NKJV). His blood wasn't spilled to camouflage sin but to cleanse it, and the indispensable response to His atoning death is repentant turning from sin. The Church needs firm convictions!

Thyatira—Counsel

> "*I have this against you: You tolerate that woman Jezebel*" (Rev. 2:20).

A wise person said, "God wants the Church in the world! Satan wants the world in the Church!" Thyatira can't tell the difference! It has a loving spirit but lacks discernment and tolerates an evil seductress referred to as "Jezebel"—a name synonymous with pagan influence. Jesus praises its loving spirit but condemns its tolerance. Some confuse love with sloppy indulgence and think any form of judgment is wrong. They're mistaken! Jesus forbade judging self-righteously or hypocritically but said to measure a tree by its fruit (Matt. 7:15-20). He never advocated permissiveness.

Postmodern culture's fundamental premise says no absolute truth exists and, by implication, God doesn't exist either—at least in any knowable form. That premise robs society of its moral compass. Permissiveness destroys homes, perverts justice and even deludes clerics. Speaking from the vacuum, contemporary Jezebels use words like *tolerant* and *inclusive* to justify ordaining sex deviates or blessing debauched relationships at church altars. Subtly seductive voices invoke social trends to excuse sin and lay standards in the dust, saying; "Well, everyone's doing it, so I guess we'll just have to accept it."

God doesn't call us to fit into a godless culture! When faith measures by biblical standards, believers become a force in converting the world. When pride measures by relative standards, the world converts them. With the spirit of counsel, our Lord urges Thyatira to hold up a standard in a world without one and warns He searches minds and hearts and repays according to one's deeds (Rev. 2:23).

Sardis—Might

> *"I know your deeds; you have a reputation of being alive, but you are dead"* (Rev. 3:1).

Jesus says Sardis is reputedly alive but actually dead. True faith is never lifeless. It isn't an abstract concept we pay lip service to but a dynamic that drives our actions. The Greek word most commonly used for it, *pistis*, implies something that is actively believed and relied upon and that sets one's course. Faith takes up a cross—perhaps in service to others or in intercessory prayer, but it characterizes those who are alive to God.

Spiritual deadness reduces faith to a lifeless abstract, and the dead do nothing! With no ministry, no vision, no outreach, no influence and no future, they simply lie wasting until progressive decay turns them to dust. Sardis is dead! Apathy has turned its faith into an empty recitation rather than a vibrant reality. Its spiritual robes have been reduced to moldy grave clothes.

God is the God of the living—not the dead. He anoints those fully alive with hearts for service, but He doesn't anoint the indifferent, the selfish or the blasé. Speaking with the spirit of might, Jesus says only a few in Sardis will walk with Him in white (Rev. 3:4). His words recall priestly ordinations in Jerusalem's temple. Since nothing blemished could enter the Holy of Holies, candidates were examined for bodily blemishes (Lev. 21:16-23). Only those free of them were given white robes as a mark of ordination.[7] Similarly, apathy and indifference are spiritual blemishes that never enter the Holy of Holies to commune intimately with God. Sardis has blemishes only repentance can remove.

Philadelphia—Knowledge

> *"I know your deeds. See, I have placed before you an open door"* (Rev. 3:8).

The test of a servant is faithfulness, and Philadelphia meets the test. Our Lord never confuses what churches do or how they look with what they are! He doesn't commend Philadelphia for the size of its congregation, the versatility of its programs and ministries or the excellence of its architecture. He doesn't measure its strategic plan, statistical growth or skillful use of analytical data relating to constituency segmentation. With the spirit of knowledge, He commends it for being faithful and promises to set before it an open door of opportunity.

Philadelphia's faithfulness is twofold. Not content to proclaim hollow words about God, it preaches a word from God and lives what it preaches! As a true and faithful people, it hasn't replaced a saving gospel with a "social gospel" or the whole counsel of God with "seeker friendly" half-truths. But doctrine alone doesn't earn our Lord's commendation. Christians in Ephesus were doctrinally sound but spiritually apathetic, and He chastened them. Christians in Philadelphia are doctrinally sound and spiritually alive, and He praises them.

Truly sound doctrine is proven by truly sound deeds. Our Lord knows Philadelphia's deeds and measures their faith by their faithfulness. The strongest do not win God's battles. The swiftest don't win His races (Eccl. 9:11). Victory belongs to the true and faithful. He promises to open doors for those qualities, and His doors lead to changed lives, changed communities and changed cultures!

Laodicea—Fear of the Lord

> *"I know your deeds, that you are neither cold nor hot. I wish you were either one or the other!"* (Rev. 3:15).

Laodicea is the only church our Lord unequivocally condemns. Condemnation is His response to sin, and this church has fallen into the sin of pride. Its name means "ruled by the people," and its failure comes from measuring itself by its own standards. Self-measurement is blind, because virtues and vices are hidden to those who possess them. Humble people can't see their own humility. They just live selflessly. Hateful people can't see their own hatefulness. They just despise others! In Laodicea, self-exaltation accompanies self-satisfaction. More enthused about feeling good than about being good, the church thinks it's rich and increased with goods when it's "*wretched, miserable, poor, blind, and naked*" (Rev. 3:17, NKJV).

Pride is an insidious sedative that deadens the soul to God, and its spell can only be broken by humility. With the spirit of the fear of the Lord, Jesus humbles Laodicea with terms relevant to the city. He tells it to buy eye salve—a product associated with the city (Rev. 3:18). He also speaks of spewing the lukewarm out of His mouth (Rev. 3:16). The city had lukewarm mineral baths. If ingested, they produced vomiting. Finally, He says to wear white robes (Rev. 3:18). Black wool was a major product of the city.

His tone is sharp and stern because this church is in danger. Its façade of self-glory must be dismantled and the brassiness of its lukewarm spirit replaced with gold tried in the fires of God's refining. Our Lord stands at its door, knocking. He is faithful to call us to Himself—even when that takes a sharp knock on life's door.

The Vision in Perspective

Then he placed his right hand on me and said:
"Do not be afraid. I am the First and the Last.
I am the Living One; I was dead, and behold I
am alive for ever and ever! And I hold the keys
of death and Hades" (Rev. 1:17-18).

This daunting vision of holiness, majesty and sovereign power echoes Sinai where fear of the divine presence kept people from the mountain (Exodus 20:18). Moses could only see the divine glory in part (Ex. 33:18-22). Divinity was veiled, and for centuries the temple's Holy of Holies was exclusive territory. The rabbis said God would destroy anyone defiling it. John knew about Sinai and once lived in awe of the temple. Confronted with the majesty of Jesus resplendent in the robes of an eternal high priest and holding the keys of the kingdom, John begins to tremble and then falls. As he does, a divine hand reaches out and an all-powerful voice speaks. The glory Moses could not see is revealed in Jesus' face, yet He says, *"Don't be afraid"* (Matt. 17:7).

Here, the echo of Sinai ceases and a contrast with it begins! Divinity reached out to open the impenetrable veil of Mt. Sinai at Mt. Calvary. Jesus is the great high priest (Heb. 4:14) whose perfect sacrifice secures access into the Holy of Holies. In Latin, the word for "priest" is *pontifex,* meaning "bridge maker," because priests reconcile people to God. Jesus is the bridge linking heaven and earth. Israel's priests made no lasting bridges to God, because sacrifices ordained in law at Sinai had to be renewed annually. The sacrifice ordained in love at Calvary forever bridges the abyss where we had fallen short of divine glory. There alone, God and man meet on common ground. Law meets grace, sin is judged, righteousness is fulfilled and a new covenant comes alive.

In this vision, we see Jesus' priestly ministry to seven churches that mirror the soul with temptations common to all of us. Drift, indifference, apathy and loss of direction test God's people whenever they fix their eyes on the world rather than on Him. Through the lens of divinity, Jesus sees with perfect insight and says with precision, "*I know your works*" (Rev. 3:1, NKJV). The voice that brought the universe into being, energized it, formed the earth, separated waters from land and created life is never one voice among others. It's never subject to any greater authority, and it gives no opinions—only truth!

Unmistakable in holiness and undeniable in power, Jesus holds the keys to death, hell and the kingdom (Rev. 1:18), but He also walks among the lampstands in spotless white as a perfect sacrifice, wearing the gold sash of a priest actively interceding (Rev. 1:13). The majesty and glory of God rest fully in the eternal bridge maker whose love casts out fear! Resplendent in the brilliance of divinity, the sovereign deity who knows our works perfectly is also the compassionate priest who's touched by our infirmities (Heb. 4:15, KJV). He invites us to come boldly to His throne (Heb. 4:16, NKJV)—and He still raises those who fall before Him.

Chapter 3

John's Second Vision—Redeemer and Judge
Part 1: Ultimate Authority

At once I was in the Spirit, and there before me was a throne in heaven with someone sitting on it... Surrounding the throne were twenty-four other thrones, and seated on them were twenty-four elders...In the center, around the throne, were four living creatures, and they were covered with eyes, in front and in back. The first living creature was like a lion, the second was like an ox, the third had a face like a man, the fourth was like a flying eagle (Rev. 4:2,4,6-7).

Recommended Reading:
Chapters 4 and 5 of Revelation

After seeing Jesus as the eternal high priest admonishing the Church, John sees the perfect Lamb of sacrifice enthroned in the heavenly temple and worshiped by cherubim, temple elders and all creation. He is one with the Father. All power is His in heaven and in earth, and all things are under His feet (Eph. 1:20-23).

This vision introduces a parallel with Passover that continues in several others. Israel's history began with the sacrifice of a lamb and deliverance from Egypt. The Church's history began with the sacrifice of "*the Lamb slain from the foundation of the world*" (Rev. 13:8, NKJV) and deliverance from sin. Jesus is the Lamb foreshadowed in the promise to Abraham and in the Passover lamb whose blood spared God's people in Egypt. He is the perfect Lamb anticipated by sacrifices in Israel's temple and the Lamb Isaiah said would bear the iniquity of us all (Isaiah 53:6). He's the Lamb John the Baptist said would take away the world's sin (John 1:29) and the author of Hebrews said "*offered Himself without spot to God*" (Heb. 9:14, NKJV). Here, He's the Lamb enthroned, and the image perfectly captures His humanity and divinity.

Jews saw the earthly temple as a replica of the heavenly one. Its altar represented God's throne. In front of it, the laver of sacred water for ceremonial washings was called the "*sea of glass, clear as crystal*" (Rev. 4:6). John sees the heavenly throne behind a crystal sea and a Presence on it surrounded in jewel-like luster, but he offers no description. In strict Jewish custom, naming God, except in prayer, is deemed too holy for human lips and a violation of the commandment to revere His name. He is only referred to as "the Holy One" or by other indirect terms. Orthodox rabbis write "G_d" but never "God."[8]

John also sees four six-winged figures or "*living creatures*" around the throne. In the earthly temple, these figures were carved on the beam above its Holy of Holies, embroidered on its veil and carved on its wall. The Old Testament refers to God as the One "*who is enthroned between the cherubim*" (1

Sam. 4:4; 2 Sam. 6:2; 1 Chron. 13:6), and these are the cherubim identified in the first and tenth chapters of Ezekiel's prophecy. One has the head of a lion, another the head of an ox, a third the head of a man and the fourth the head of an eagle (Ezek. 1:10). The lion represented everything noble; the ox, everything strong; the man, everything wise and the eagle, everything swift. By implication, everything noble, strong, wise or swift in creation hovers around God's throne, forever testifying to His glory.

John's vision of twenty-four thrones also recalls temple worship. During the year, priestly ministries rotated among twenty-four groups made up of priests or Levites—two for each of Israel's twelve tribes. On high holy days, all twenty-four attended, since all tribes were to be fully represented during such occasions. Ismar Elbogen of Hebrew Union College explains:

> Priests and Levites were divided into twenty-four groups. One week every half year, each of these would send a mission to Jerusalem to stand over the sacrifice. During this week of service, the representatives of the people would hold four services every day, morning, additional, afternoon and at the closing of the temple gates. These consisted of Torah reading and prayers.[9]

On the Day of Atonement or Yom Kippur, prostration was common during solemn prayers. As the cherubim praise God, John sees twenty-four elders prostrated in submission, affirming Jesus as

supremely worthy of undivided adoration and service (Rev. 4:10-11).

Opening the Scroll

*Then I saw in the right hand of him who sat on
the throne a scroll with writing on both sides
and sealed with seven seals. And I saw a
mighty angel proclaiming in a loud voice, "Who
is worthy to break the seals and open the
scroll?"* (Rev. 5:1,2).

As the cosmic stage is set in the heavenly temple,
John sees the eternal drama of salvation. Before the
cherubim and elders, an angel cries in a loud voice,
"Who is worthy to...open the scroll?" In Judaism, the
Torah scroll inscribed with Scripture's books of law
is so revered it can't be printed by machine and must
be handwritten.[10] If damaged beyond use, it's set
aside and given proper burial in a Jewish cemetery.
In synagogues, it not only symbolizes the letter of
God's law but also His mind and heart, and only persons of upright character are deemed worthy to open
it. Rabbi Jonathan Sachs explains:

> The holiest object in Judaism is a scroll of the law.
> It symbolizes some of Judaism's deepest
> beliefs...that God is to be found in words, that
> these words are to be found in the Torah, and that
> they form the basis of the covenant—the bond of
> love—between God and the Jewish people.[11]

As an early Jewish Christian, John sees the Torah scroll as a bond of love and as the symbol of righteous authority. Small wonder he weeps when it is irrevocably sealed! His tears reflect the human dilemma. Nicholas Berdyaev, Russian thinker during revolutionary times, said human history is an ongoing tragedy. Nothing man builds endures! In mute testimony, all the great civilizations of yesterday lie silent in dust.

Tragically detached from the reason he was created, man lies across an abyss, short of the glory of God. From Eden onward, his unrelenting hostility to God's unrelenting love has reaped a perpetually wretched harvest. Groping desperately, he looks for saviors, making demagogues of history's darkest figures, and then weeps helplessly as wars, suicide bombings, terrorism, rapes, kidnappings, robberies and murders proliferate, ultimately bringing down every civilization. Fools claim man has outgrown his need for God, but history's continuing carnage undoes their presumption and makes a counterfeit of their pride.

Albert Einstein, named "Man of the 20th Century" by *Time Magazine*, was very disillusioned after his discovery of atomic power produced a bomb that instantly incinerated tens of thousands.[12] As the century's most brilliant mind, he said:

> The release of atom power has changed everything except our way of thinking. If only I had known, I should have become a watchmaker. Technological progress is like putting an axe in the hands of a pathological criminal.

When our best technologies only increase our capacity for human slaughter, humanity weeps along with John. Its tears flow on battlefields, in courtrooms, ghettos, prisons and all the arenas of misery where no bond of love binds men to God or each other.

Lion and Lamb

Then I saw a Lamb, looking as if it had been slain, standing in the center of the throne, encircled by the four living creatures and the elders (Rev. 5:6).

John's tears are dried as he hears a voice saying, "*The Lion of the tribe of Judah, the Root of David, has prevailed to open the scroll*" (Rev. 5:5, NKJV). The term *Lion of Judah* is a synonym for "righteous judge" and originated when a dying Jacob called his son Judah "*a lion's whelp*" (Genesis 49:9, NKJV), saying, "*The scepter will not depart from Judah, nor the ruler's staff from between his feet, until he comes to whom it belongs*" (Gen. 49:10).

The *root of David* also means "righteous judge." In Jeremiah, we read, "*The days are coming*," declares the LORD, "*when I will raise up to David a righteous Branch, a King who will reign wisely and do what is just and right in the land*" (Jer. 23:5).

Similarly, Isaiah prophesied:

A shoot will come up from the stump of Jesse; from his roots a Branch will bear fruit. The

*Spirit of the LORD will rest on him—the Spirit
of wisdom and of understanding, the Spirit of
counsel and of power, the Spirit of knowledge
and of the fear of the LORD—and he will
delight in the fear of the LORD. He will not
judge by what he sees with his eyes, or decide
by what he hears with his ears; but with righteousness...He will strike the earth with the
rod of his mouth; with the breath of his lips he
will slay the wicked* (Isa. 11:1-4).

The victory of the "Lion of Judah" means righteousness has been vindicated, but the victor isn't a
powerful warrior resplendent in battle dress.
Instead, it's a sacrificial Lamb worthy to open the
scroll by the shedding of its blood. If our Lord were
only the Lion of righteous judgment, sinful humanity
would be condemned. If He were only a Lamb of sacrifice, the atonement would be a mere indulgence.
He is both! As Lion, He judges righteously. As Lamb,
He provides the perfect sacrifice for sin. Revelation is
defined by these two images—righteous judge and
perfect sacrifice. In all that follows, our Lord is either
Redeemer or Judge.

John notes that the Lamb takes the scroll in its
right hand. In Jewish tradition, holding scrolls in the
left hand is a sacrilege. As John watches, cherubim
and elders seize harps and bowls of incense. Its
smoke symbolizes the prayers of the people rising to
God (Rev. 5:8). Seizing the bowls means the Lamb's
sacrifice has met humanity's heart cry, and heaven
begins to sing:

"You are worthy to take the scroll and to open its seals, because you were slain, and with your blood you purchased men for God from every tribe and language and people and nation. You have made them to be a kingdom and priests to serve our God, and they will reign on the earth" (Rev. 5:9,10).

As John listens, millions of angels join the choir loudly singing: *"Worthy is the Lamb, who was slain, to receive power and wealth and wisdom and strength and honor and glory and praise!"* (Rev. 5:12).

In a glorious crescendo, all creation joins in. *"To him who sits on the throne and to the Lamb be praise and honor and glory and power, for ever and ever!"* (Rev. 5:13).

When their song ends, the four living creatures say "Amen" and the elders prostrate themselves before the Lamb (Rev. 5:14). *Amen* was used as a response in temple worship only after careful consideration, to support a blessing or affirm a solemn vow. Prostration and the use of "Amen" together show unequivocal submission and service.

The Vision in Perspective

Then I saw a Lamb, looking as if it had been slain, standing in the center of the throne (Rev. 5:6).

As Revelation's keystone, this vision exalts the Lamb's sacrifice on Calvary as time and eternity's ultimate statement. The picture of Him standing in the center of the throne has but one meaning—Jesus, the Lamb, is God. With some of Scripture's loftiest Christology, John offers three comparisons proving Jesus' lordship over angels, the elders of Israel and all creation.

His superiority to angels was also expounded in the book of Hebrews at length. Why? New Testament evidence proves Jesus' resurrection was known throughout Jerusalem. Perhaps some tried to explain it by making Him an angelic being—supernatural in character but less than divine. This vision proves Him superior! The cherubim, representing everything noble, swift, strong or wise in creation, aren't worthy to open the scroll. Jesus is!

Jesus is also superior to the elders of Israel who can't open the scroll. His supremacy over them proves the call of Abraham, the exodus, the covenant of law, the prophets and all the elements of Israel's history had only one purpose—to prepare for One who by shedding His blood could prove worthy to open the scroll. Israel was never an end in itself. It was a channel through which God revealed His Son, and its sacrifices were incomplete types pointing to the perfect Lamb of sacrifice by whom God would reconcile the world to Himself. Jesus, not Israel, is the center of history.

Heresies diminishing Him as the fulfillment of promise and claiming special status for Israel cursed the early Church. To refute them, Paul traced Israel's history to its source and told the Galatians the promises made by God to Abraham would be fulfilled in Jesus—not in Israel:

> *The promises were spoken to Abraham and to his seed. The Scripture does not say "and to seeds," meaning many people, but "and to your seed," meaning one person, who is Christ...You are all sons of God through faith in Christ Jesus, or all of you who were baptized into Christ have clothed yourselves with Christ. There is neither Jew nor Greek, slave nor free, male nor female, for you are all one in Christ Jesus* (Gal. 3:16,26-28).

His letter to Ephesus said the mystery of God is accomplished in Christ and barriers between Jew and Gentile are broken down "*throughout all generations, for ever and ever*" (Eph. 3:21). Since they're gone forever, Israel has no "favored nation" status!

In his epistle to the Romans, Paul makes a pivotal argument for justification that's generally seen as the heart of salvation theology. Citing Abraham as the example of justifying faith (Rom. 4), Paul says Christians living by faith are the true Israel and Abraham's real descendants (Rom. 9:8,30-31). That doesn't mean that God has forever spurned Jews who reject the Messiah. Paul says they can be "*grafted in*" if they don't continue in unbelief but turn to Jesus in repentance (Rom. 11:23). To be "grafted in" means to be joined to something living. Unbelievers—whether Jew or Gentile—miss the new and living way of salvation through faith. Paul anticipates some Jews will find it and concludes his argument in a play on words, saying, "*And so all Israel will be saved*" (Rom. 11:26). Consistent with his view throughout the epistle, "*all*

Israel" refers to the spiritual Israel of faith—not the natural one defined by race.

This vision correctly centers everything around our Lord's death and atonement. The cross is the axis of history, but heresies making it a mere parenthesis in time still persist in insisting that the Jewish nation will be completely restored. These heresies usually misinterpret Paul's reference to "grafting in" as a resurrection of the old covenant. Since Jesus' blood is "*the blood of the everlasting covenant*" (Heb. 13:20, NKJV), it applies forever. The old covenant is forever dead, and salvation through Christ is no parenthesis. His cross is the measure of mankind, and it determines mastery of the scroll. That's why Israel's elders bow before the Lamb!

The Lamb is also Lord of all creation. By His will the world was created, and it exists only at His pleasure. Its beauty testifies to Him, but it can't reveal Him. At best, it's an altar to an unknown god. If God's handiwork doesn't reveal Him, our handiwork won't either! Idols carved in wood or stone shed no blood for the sins of the world and open no scrolls. Philosophy and science grope blindly for mastery of the universe, only to confront their own inevitable limitations. Left to ourselves, we cannot find God by searching. The scroll is sealed to human inquiry.

The heart of the old covenant—symbolized by the scroll—was the great commandment to love God and neighbor selflessly (Matt. 22:36-40). Nothing less can dry the world's tears and bring the righteousness of a holy God to human hearts, but who is worthy to open such a scroll? Only one life and death has perfectly expressed love that will pay any price for God and man; He alone is supremely worthy to open it. Superior to angels, the elders of Israel and all created things, He is Lord, and He alone can reveal Himself to human hearts. He is not a way, a truth or a life! He is *the* way, the truth and the life! (John 14:6). He stands, incomparably, with supreme and absolute authority as the one and only eternal God who for our sakes became flesh (John 1:14). His cross is history's dividing line and its only hope. Angels in heaven stand in awe of it. Jew and Gentile stand equal beneath it, and all creation is judged by it. The Lamb is our Redeemer. The Lion of Judah is our righteous Judge. He has prevailed, and the scroll is in His hands!

Chapter 4

John's Second Vision—Redeemer and Judge
Part 2: Seeing the Alternatives

I watched as the Lamb opened the first of the seven seals (Rev. 6:1).

Recommended Reading:
Chapters 6 and 7 of Revelation

John's vision of a sacrificial lamb recalls Passover, and his visions of horsemen and plagues extend the parallel between that event and the life of the Church. To Jews, Passover is history's defining event. They were enslaved for 400 years when God called Moses to seek their release (Exod. 12:40-41). Pharaoh resisted, and plagues were visited on him to break his resolve (Exod. 7-9). These grew in intensity until God sent the death angel to Egypt's first-born sons (Exod. 12:29-30). Pharaoh's will was broken, and he freed the Jews but later relented and sent horsemen to recapture them (Exod. 14:5-9). They should have easily overtaken the Israelites, but God overruled. Horses and riders drowned in the sea that the Israelites miraculously passed through on foot (Exod. 14:21-29). In a strange irony, horsemen symbolizing Pharaoh's power became symbols of judgment and destruction.[13]

Passover models judgment and redemption and shapes John's perspective deeply. As a young boy, he likely traveled to Jerusalem for three annual "pilgrimage festivals"—Passover, Pentecost and the Feast of Tabernacles anticipated in Isaiah's words:

> On this mountain the LORD Almighty will prepare a feast of rich food for all peoples, a banquet of aged wine—best of meats and the finest of wines. On this mountain he will destroy the shroud that enfolds all peoples, the sheet that covers all nations; he will swallow up death forever. The Sovereign LORD will wipe away the tears from all faces; he will remove the disgrace of his people from all the earth (Isa. 25:6-8).

The feasts coincided with the seasons. Rabbis taught God regularly took humanity's measure at each new season, citing Psalm 33:15 (KJV): "He fashioneth their hearts alike; he considereth all their works." The way of the transgressor was hard, but the end of the righteous was peace.[14] Passover's promise of righteous judgment was celebrated with readings, including Lamentations 3:66, "Pursue them in anger and destroy them from under the heavens of the LORD," Psalm 79:6, "Pour out your wrath on the nations that do not acknowledge you, on the kingdoms that do not call on your name" and Psalm 69:25, "May their place be *deserted; let there be no one to dwell in their tents.*"

As a Jewish Christian, John saw Jesus as the true Passover Lamb and knew judgment or redemption would define our ultimate fate. As a prisoner, John saw the wicked butcher the righteous and swagger over their corpses. Some of his fellow believers had paid for their faith with their lives. A gospel that didn't judge evil was no gospel, but John sees a distinction between the havoc sin brings and God's final judgment.

As Jesus, the true Passover Lamb, opens the scroll, the moral lesson of Passover becomes universal. John sees an insane world in the image of horsemen wreaking destruction but also sees a multitude standing in pure white before the throne of God. He then sees a final judgment on all sin and unrighteousness that leaves the redeemed unscathed. The contrast shows the relative fates of an order that is doomed and of a people washed in the blood of the Lamb.

Four Horsemen

I heard one of the four living creatures say in a voice like thunder, "Come!" I looked, and there before me was a white horse! (Rev. 6:1-2).

As the Lamb opens the seals, John sees four horsemen, representing the corruption of a fallen world. In a world brutalized by ruthless Roman power, he sees the universal truth of humanity's interminable inclination to exploitation and destruction.

The first rider, on a white horse, symbolizes conquest (Rev. 6:2). The second, on a red horse, has a large sword, symbolizing war (Rev. 6:4). The third, on a black horse, symbolizes unjust exploitation. Wheat commands a day's wages and barley cost three days' wages. Oil and wine are reserved for the few (Rev. 6:5,6). The fourth rider, on a pale horse, symbolizes death—by sword, famine, plagues and even wild beasts (Rev. 6:8).

One bitter legacy of the fall is man's predisposition to self-destruction. Sooner or later, his lip service to lasting peace and economic justice is undone by competition for wealth and power, and arms and force determine the outcome. Those who've scoured the ashes of Hiroshima, smelled the gas ovens of the third Reich, walked the killing fields of Cambodia or dug up mass graves in Bosnia have seen the hoofprints of earth's apocalyptic horsemen. Conquests, wars and deprivation constantly circle the globe, and death's pale horse always follows them.

The Blood of the Martyrs

When he opened the fifth seal, I saw under the altar the souls of those who had been slain because of the word of God and the testimony they had maintained. They called out in a loud voice, "How long, Sovereign Lord, holy and true, until you judge the inhabitants of the earth and avenge our blood?" Then each of them was given a white robe, and they were told to wait a little longer, until the number of their fellow servants and brothers who were to be killed as they had been was completed" (Rev. 6:9-11).

As early Christians under Roman rule knew only too well, earth's carnage often victimizes the righteous. After seeing the four horsemen of oppression, John sees the souls of martyrs under the altar crying out, "*How long...until you avenge our blood?*" Perhaps John recalled the question in Zechariah where an angel asked God how long until He would show mercy on the fallen cities of Jerusalem and Judah.

He must have recalled the 29th chapter of Exodus. Blood was sprinkled under the altar during the dedication of Aaron's sons—Israel's first priests. John sees Christians as a royal priesthood in a world that beheads them, crucifies them and has them devoured by beasts. The blood consecrating the floor of Rome's arenas sprinkles heaven's altar as a sacrifice, and the voices of the slain cry out, "How long?" John hears no easy reply. Our Lord doesn't exempt the martyrs from mortality or immediately avenge their deaths. He gives them white robes and tells them to wait.

God's priorities differ from ours! Jesus said the world would bring tribulation but to be of good cheer (John 16:33, NKJV). Faith's object is God, and perfect faith is perfectly submissive. It prizes pure hearts more than pleasant circumstances, and it doesn't try to manipulate God by using semantic confessions as mantras to bring Him to heel. The white robe of faith worn by believers enters Gethsemane with "*Thy will be done*" (Matt. 26:42, KJV) and never with "My will be done!" and it's proven by what it accepts rather than what it receives.

Who Can Stand?

Then the kings of the earth, the princes, the generals, the rich, the mighty and every slave and every free man hid in caves and among the rocks of the mountains. They called to the mountains and the rocks, "Fall on us and hide us from the face of him who sits on the throne and from the wrath of the Lamb! For the great day of their wrath has come, and who can stand?" (Rev. 6:15-17).

As the sixth seal is broken, John is reminded creation is finite and foresees the day the universe will vanish at the sound of a divine command. At Passover, God's righteous judgment stripped Pharaoh of his power. In parallel images that must have given hope to an early Church facing Roman persecution and martyrdom, John sees God's final judgment sweep away kings, empires, princes, generals, the wealthy and the powerful. Like Pharaoh's horsemen, they vanish in a maelstrom of destruction, shrieking, "*Who can stand?*" The question is answered as a redeemed multitude "*from every nation, tribe, people and language*" (Rev. 7:9) stands before the throne in a celebration that echoes Israel's joy after crossing the Red Sea. The contrast confronts us with life's ultimate choice—judgment or redemption.

From Every Tribe and Nation

From the tribe of Judah, 12,000 were sealed,

from the tribe of Reuben 12,000, from the tribe of Gad 12,000, from the tribe of Asher 12,000, from the tribe of Naphtali 12,000, from the tribe of Manasseh 12,000, from the tribe of Simeon 12,000, from the tribe of Levi 12,000, from the tribe of Issachar 12,000, from the tribe of Zebulon 12,000, from the tribe of Joseph 12,000, from the tribe of Benjamin 12,000. After this I looked and there before me was a great multitude that no one could count, from every nation, tribe, people and language, standing before the throne and in front of the Lamb. They were wearing white robes and were holding palm branches in their hands (Rev. 7:5-9).

At Passover, the children of Israel danced on the shores of the Red Sea after escaping Egypt (Exod. 15:20). Extending the parallel, John sees a multitude standing in holy celebration. Sheltering angels stand at earth's four corners, sealing and sparing them from destruction (Rev. 7:1-3). He describes the crowd as 144,000 people (Rev. 7:4). Perhaps the number traces back to Pentecost, where 12 groups of 10 made up 120 souls in the upper room (Acts 1:15). This scene grows that number to 12 x 12 multiplied by 10 x 10 x 10, or an infinite multitude standing in triumph, redeemed from the world's corruption and spared from its judgment. John names them with an inaccurate list of Israel's tribes, placing Judah, the tribe of Jesus, in first position instead of Reuben and omitting Ephraim and Dan. He knew Israel's tribes perfectly, but his list draws on the chronicler's record of Israel's military camps—not its tribes. In fact, why name tribes at all? Seven centuries before John, ten tribes disappeared under the Assyrian invasion, and tribal identities within Judaism waned.[15] Subsequent intermarriage among tribes made them irrelevant.

John's inaccurate list of tribes is not the old Israel but the new one washed in the blood of the Lamb. In a later vision, he describes the host of 144,000 as *"redeemed from among men, being first-fruits to God and to the Lamb"* (Rev. 14:4, NKJV)—another New Testament term for the Church. New Testament authors often applied terms associated with Israel to the Church. In Romans, Paul said, *"For not all who are descended from Israel are Israel"* (Rom. 9:6) and *"It is not the natural children who are God's children"* (Rom. 9:8). Peter called the Church a *"a chosen generation, a royal priesthood, a holy nation"* (1 Pet. 2:9, NKJV), and James called it *"the twelve tribes which are scattered abroad"* (Jas. 1:1, NKJV).

The happy prospect of a multitude standing is a subtle reference to Jewish custom. During the Day of Atonement, observant Jews stand in synagogues individually and collectively, as if before God, to give an account.[16] Rabbis preach sermons on personal responsibility, symbolized by standing on that holiest of Jewish holy days.

John's vision raises questions. Who stands before God's throne serving Him day and night in His holy place? Who are these over whom His tent is spread wide and who hunger and thirst no more? Who are these living with the Lamb in their midst and drinking from springs of living water? Who are these whose tears are dried by God Himself? Who are these with robes made white in the blood of the Lamb? Who are these who stand when creation is crumbling? Surely they're the new Israel—the Church!

Their white robes signify atonement (Rev. 7:9), their "*springs of living water*" (Rev. 7:17) is the Holy Spirit and their palm branches are a messianic symbol (Rev. 7:9). On certain holy days, Jews waved palms vertically in four directions, signifying heaven's union with earth's four corners.

They did so on Palm Sunday, crying "*Hosanna,*" meaning "Save now," and chanting Psalm 118's messianic blessing on the one "*who comes in the name of the Lord!*" (Matt. 21:9). That psalm crescendos in the words "*save us*" (Ps. 118:25). This white-robed multitude waving palms is a picture of salvation as the redeemed from earth's four corners praise the One who washed them in His blood.

The Vision in Perspective

"*He will lead them to springs of living water. And God will wipe away every tear from their eyes*" (Rev. 7:17).

Jesus, the triumphal Lamb, holds the scroll that condemns sin and redeems the righteous. Therefore, the ultimate realities of our world are an inevitable judgment on sin and the possibility of redemption through the blood of the Lamb. This vision repeats the moral lesson of Passover by contrasting them.

In this scene, sin faces two judgments! The first is the self-imposed havoc it makes of human affairs—as symbolized by four horsemen. Man's fall in Eden plunged him into a world that's its own worst enemy. Created to glorify God, he seeks to glorify himself. Pomp and presumption drive his actions but never satisfy his soul. With self-interest as his ultimate value, his eternal inclination to exploit and destroy regularly dispatches horsemen to bloody the annals of time, spilling even the blood of the righteous on the ground. Apart from the judgment humanity imposes on itself, God will bring another. On a great and final day, history will close, and He'll roll back the sky as a scroll, dropping stars from it like figs from trees. That day of ultimate judgment is shown by the dark specter of once powerful figures shrieking as creation implodes.

In Egypt, Pharaoh cast a long shadow of power and influence. Like him, many people cast similar shadows and live obsessing about the length of their shadows. Unfortunately for them, shadows are illusory and lack any real substance. Egypt's horsemen personifying Pharaoh's power and might proved to be only a shadow cast in time, and time is finite. Life's ultimate reality is our accountability to an eternal God. Earth's shadows of influence will someday vanish like Pharaoh's horsemen in a wave of destruction.

If Pharaoh's horsemen personified judgment, the children of Israel were pictures of redemption. They were only defenseless slaves in Egypt but were spared from death and destruction by the blood of lambs. Interestingly, Passover's seal of blood may be an enigma for traditional rabbis since Israel had no covenant, sacrifices or consecrated alters in Egypt. Offering a mechanical explanation of Israel's deliverance, one might conclude blood on the doorposts caused God to view Jewish homes in Egypt as altars. As such, they'd be divine territory sheltered from death's destruction.

Applying the lesson of Passover to the Church, John sees the meaning of a host standing triumphantly on holy ground. The lambs slain for Passover anticipated a greater promise fulfilled on a bleak afternoon two thousand years later when the blood of *"the Lamb slain from the foundation of the world"* (Rev. 13:8) transformed a rocky promontory outside Jerusalem into an altar. On that day, a forgotten hill called Golgotha became divine territory. This insignificant rise with its strange skull-like rock face now shelters redeemed multitudes too large to number. With robes washed white in the blood spilled there, they stand, shouting the high praises of the Lamb while death only passes over and sheltering angels seal off destruction.

Chapter 5

John's Third Vision—The Yoke of Hell

When he opened the seventh seal, there was silence in heaven for about half an hour. And I saw the seven angels who stand before God, and to them were given seven trumpets (Rev. 8:1-2).

Recommended Reading:
Chapters 8 and 9 of Revelation

John's third vision extends the parallel with Passover as seven angels sound trumpets announcing plagues. God sent plagues to call Pharaoh to repentance, and these symbolize His call to humanity to repent.

Egypt personified godlessness, as typified by Pharaoh's reply to Moses, *"Who is the LORD, that I should obey him and let Israel go? I do not know the LORD and I will not let Israel go"* (Exod. 5:2).

Pharaoh lived under the illusion that he had complete freedom to do as he pleased. Mortality nullifies absolute freedom, but the ungodly ignore that. As supreme ruler, Pharaoh was worshiped. By human measurement, he was invincible until subjected to forces beyond his control. Then he began to lose his freedom to calamities, from which Jews were spared. The tyrant who neither knew nor cared about the eternal God was stripped of his mastery and left helpless.

Jews and Egyptians saw the plagues of Passover differently. To Jews, they were the first steps of deliverance. Their servitude was in marked contrast to the Egyptians' mastery, and each Jew is taught Israel's liberation was a personal triumph—not simply a revered event of history. Twice daily, observant Jews still recite this prayer: "I am the Lord your God, who has taken you from the land of Egypt to be for you a God; I am the Lord your God."

Jews, indebted to God for deliverance from Egypt, are to honor Him with their lives. Rabbis call this "accepting the yoke of heaven." The Mishna explains:

> *In every generation, a person must see himself as if he had left Egypt, as it says, 'You shall tell your child on that day, saying, It is because of what God did for me when I went free from Egypt.' We are therefore obliged to thank, praise, extol, glorify, elevate, exalt, bless, honor and magnify the One who performed all these miracles for our forefathers and us* (Pesachim 116b).

Pharaoh's rejection of God was his undoing, and, for Egyptians, the plagues became the yoke of hell. Like Pharaoh, those who boast they "know not the Lord" face restrictions on their freedom that call them to repent. Life inevitably forces us to choose the yoke of heaven or of hell, and the plagues of this vision aren't scenes of senseless devastation in some "end times" scenario. The first four represent the constraints of man's fallen condition in every age. He also faces Satan's hatred, and the fifth and sixth plagues show the twin disasters of satanic deception and eternal death.

John's priestly training is evident throughout this passage. First, he notes silence in the heavenly temple. This recalls worship in the earthly one. After a wretched Babylonian captivity, Israel repudiated all forms of idolatrous worship—especially its attempt to orchestrate fervor through repeating magical incantations and chants. Jesus, Himself, spoke of the "*vain repetitions as the heathen do*" (Matt. 6:7, NKJV). To avoid such practices, Israel developed a profound reverence for silence and conducted worship in the temple accordingly. Yehezkel Kaufmann explains:

> In the pagan world in general, word and incantation were integral parts of the cult; act was accompanied by speech...[In the Jerusalem temple] all the various acts of the priest are performed in silence...Silence is an intuitive expression of the priestly desire to fashion a non pagan cult.[17]

After sacrifices, priests burned incense in a golden censer symbolizing the prayers ascending to God. During this "time of incense," worshipers fell to their knees spreading their hands in deep, prolonged silent prayers after which the priest cast coals from a censer onto the earth, symbolizing God's answer.

In John's vision, an angel offers incense at the throne (Rev. 8:3-4). Heaven falls silent as the angel then hurls coals onto the earth. Peals of thunder and lightning shatter the silence! (Rev. 8:5). An earthquake follows, and six angels sound trumpets, introducing plagues. Importantly, there are seven angels (Rev. 8:6) but only six sound trumpets (Rev. 8:7-9:13).

The rabbis said "seven angels of the Presence" stood in a place of honor near God to be immediately dispatched in His service. Jewish apocryphal books, such as *Tobit*, had a well-developed angelology referring to Uriel, Raphael, Raguel, Michael, Sariel, Gabriel and Remiel. Mr. Kaufmann reviews the teaching that shaped John's imagery:

> Destructive agents are sometimes styled by terms that may be taken as proper nouns; "negef" (plague), "mashhith" (destroyer), "qeteb miri" (bitter destruction), "neshef" (fiery bolt), and the like"...It is of crucial significance that all destructive agents, "neshef" included, do not constitute a domain opposing YHWH; like the rest of the angels, they are His messengers only.[18]

The angels John sees are destructive agents, or *negef*, calling man to repentance. The trumpets he hears are *shofar* made of rams' horns that signaled Israel's major events and still have symbolic meaning for Jews. In his *Guide to Jewish Religious Practice*, Rabbi Isaac Klein cites ten points in an ancient teaching about them:

1. The sound of the Shofar is analogous to the trumpet blasts which announce the coronation of a king...

2. Rosh Hashanah [New Year's] is the first of Ten Days of Penitence, and the Shofar is sounded to stir our consciences...

3. The Shofar is reminiscent of God's revelation at Sinai, which was accompanied by the sounding of a Shofar...

4. The sound of the Shofar is reminiscent of the exhortations of the prophets, whose voices rang out like a Shofar...

5. The Shofar reminds us of the destruction of the temple, and calls upon us to strive for Israel's renewal in freedom and in fellowship with God.

6. The Shofar, since it is a ram's horn, is reminiscent of the ram offered as a sacrifice by Abraham...

7. The Shofar urges us to feel humble before God's majesty...

8. The Shofar is a reminder of the Day of Final Judgment calling upon all men and all nations to prepare themselves for God's scrutiny of their deeds.

9. The Shofar foreshadows the jubilant procla-
   mation of freedom...

10. The Shofar foreshadows the end of the pre-
    sent world order and the inauguration of
    God's reign of righteousness...[19]

More succinctly, trumpets celebrated God's faithfulness and power and also summoned the people to
repentance. In the earthly temple, their notes signaled divine acceptance of the sacrifices and an
answer to the prayers of the people. At Rosh
Hashanah or New Year's, seven trumpet blasts her-
alded seven recitations of Psalm 47, in which God's
name occurs seven times, praising creation. John's
readers would readily associate trumpet blasts with
the power of God.

On the last of the ten days of penitence noted by
Rabbi Klein—the annual Day of Atonement or Yom
Kippur—the temple doors closed after the final service. On all other days, they remained open but were
closed that day to remind people of the need to repent
according to the covenant. The sound of the shofar
was a warning to come and pray while opportunity
remained. John's trumpets and plagues are powerful
warnings. Like Pharaoh, fallen man faces inescapable
constraints on his freedom that call him to repent.

Four Plagues—Disaster, Thirst, Wormwood and Darkness

*The first angel sounded his trumpet, and there
came hail and fire mixed with blood...The*

second angel sounded his trumpet, and something like a huge mountain, all ablaze, was thrown into the sea. A third of the sea turned into blood...The third angel sounded his trumpet, and a great star, blazing like a torch, fell from the sky on a third of the rivers and on the springs of water—the name of the star is Wormwood...The fourth angel sounded his trumpet...A third of the day was without light, and also a third of the night (Rev. 8:7,8,10,12).

The first plague announced by the angels combines hail, fire and blood, much like one of hail and fire in Egypt (Exod. 9:23-24, NKJV). John's reference to blood may echo Joel's prophecy of the moon being turned to blood (Joel 2:31). The illogical mixture of hail, fire and blood shows nature in rebellion. Man's fall cursed creation, and it groans for redemption. God intended man for Eden, but sin consigned him to a world where natural disasters happen. These destructive agents do not entirely destroy him but remind him of his mortality.

In the second plague, one-third of the sea turns to blood. In Egypt, Moses stretched forth his rod and the Nile's waters turned to blood (Exod. 7:20). Egypt depended on those waters, and their loss was a calamity. John sees man's dilemma, trying to quench the thirst of his soul apart from God, and likened it to the plague of undrinkable blood. Because this plague symbolizes life's inevitable constraints and not earth's final destruction, only one-third of the sea is undrinkable.

The third plague is a fiery bolt or "great star" (*neshef*) falling from the sky, turning waters to wormwood (*qeteb miri*). In nature, wormwood is a plant species called "artemisia," known for its bitter taste. In Scripture, it symbolizes punishment for idolatry. Moses warned the children of Israel against idols of wood, stone, silver or gold lest they be given wormwood to drink (Deut. 29:14-19). Centuries later, Jeremiah warned Israel would drink poisonous wormwood for worshiping Baal (Jer. 9:13-15).

Modern man worships an unholy trinity of wealth, sex and self, but these idols offer only bitter wormwood. The god of materialism is a respecter of persons and blesses only the prosperous, but in due course their riches possess them and they become disillusioned. Man's god of sex is also a mocker. Wanton lifestyles reap a bitter harvest of divorce, disease and disenchantment. His god of self is the most insidious deceiver!

In the fourth plague, darkness falls on the earth for one-third of the day and night. Before Passover, a plague of darkness mocked Egyptian idolatry. The people worshiped the sun, but darkness surrounded them (Exod. 10:21-23). Since it didn't affect the Israelites, some conclude it wasn't an external event but a failure in the eyes of the Egyptians. Similarly, man's unregenerate state is a failure that blinds him to the light of God's love.

These plagues prove he lives in an imperfect world that can prove hostile. His thirst isn't satisfied by what it offers. His idols have feet of clay, and his grasp is drastically foreshortened. These constraints restrict his freedom and call him to repentance. The fifth and sixth plagues represent Satan's attack on him. To distinguish them, John sees a flying eagle announce them (Rev. 8:13).

The Fifth and Sixth Plagues—
Demonic Locusts, Angels of Death

When he opened the Abyss, smoke rose from it like the smoke from a gigantic furnace. The sun and sky were darkened by the smoke from the Abyss. And out of the smoke locusts came down upon the earth...During those days men will seek death, but will not find it; they will long to die, but death will elude them...And the four angels who had been kept ready for this very hour and day and month and year were released to kill a third of mankind (Rev. 9:2,3,6,15).

In Scripture, as in life, God is absolutely sovereign. He has no equals and no rivals. In some ancient religions, gods were good or evil and the universe was the sphere in which everlasting power struggles took place. Christianity holds no such prospect. Evil is attributable to rebellion in heaven against God by Satan—an infinitely lesser being who fell from heaven before time. Because his fall preceded time, this vision does not depict a future event.

As the fifth angel sounds his trumpet, a star falls from heaven and is given a key to the abyss. In Jewish tradition, a "star" refers to a spirit and the abyss is a nether region designated as a place of judgment and punishment. The fallen spirit is Satan or *Abbadon*, the Hebrew name for "destroyer." *Appollyon* is the Greek equivalent (Rev. 9:11).

As John watches, he releases a plague of locusts. In biblical times locusts always meant destruction and hardship, but these bear no resemblance to any natural plague. They don't harm earth's vegetation or those bearing God's seal but torment the rest of the world for five months—about the normal life expectancy of a locust (Rev. 9:5). What kind of locust harms no vegetation and spares people selectively? What evils from the pit of hell attack only unbelievers? What does Satan unloose but endless lies to deceive and damn those who prefer darkness to light? His role, attested to fifty-two times in Scripture, is as an accuser and slanderer. He can't master nature or earth's vegetation—representing God's provision for man. His lies don't deceive the children of light who do not walk in darkness, but they victimize unbelievers! In a later vision, John warns of those who enter hell along with "*the devil that deceived them*" (Revelation 20:10, KJV).

Unbelief is a delusion that begins with defiance and ends with despair. Despite the fall, man still bears the disfigured image of God and instinctively seeks life's purpose, order and meaning. His search drives the microcosmic quests of science and the macrocosmic questions of philosophy. Why do things happen? Knowing they happen is information. Knowing why is mastery. Surely life has a point! Why are we here? Atheism must remain silent! Since it denies an intelligent Creator and makes life the result of a random accident in space, it can neither ask nor answer questions of purpose. Life is a question for which God, alone, is the answer!

A death wish often follows a sense of meaninglessness. Notably, organizations that promote atheism send no missionaries to aid the needy or deprived but champion initiatives to slaughter the unborn or promote euthanasia. How deceived is man when the destroyer convinces him that life is his enemy and death is an elusive prize?

At Passover, the last plague visited on an unrepentant Pharaoh occurred when the angel of death claimed Egypt's eldest sons. In a spiritual context, sin's ultimate wage is death, and Revelation's sixth plague points to a final payday. The Euphrates River was once Israel's furthest boundary, and the image of four angels crossing it and releasing 200 million destroyers to slaughter one-third of mankind (Rev. 9:16) is a picture of death's universality. The number of 200 million combines ten, meaning finality, with seven, meaning completeness. Ten multiplied to the seventh power, doubled for good measure, equals 200 million. It's appointed unto man once to die (Heb. 9:27), and death's angels visit every soul. Sadly, even that sobering reality seldom brings repentance. Rebellion is hardened in the furnace of defiance and shaped on the anvil of denial.

The antidote to Satan's deception is the "seal of God," and this vision extracts the term from the Jewish Day of Atonement's final service where all prayers began with a plea to God to seal His people. Joseph Heinemann explains:

On the Day of Atonement, the formula "inscribe us in the book of life" and its equivalents are exchanged for "seal us into the book of life" indicating that with the day drawing to its end, the divine decree is about to be made final.[20]

The Holy Spirit seals Christians! His presence and guidance is their unshakeable defense against the wiles of the devil. As Paul said to Timothy;

"Nevertheless, God's solid foundation stands firm, sealed with this inscription: 'The Lord knows those who are his'" (2 Tim. 2:19).

The Vision in Perspective

Nor did they repent of their murders, their magic arts, their sexual immorality or their thefts (Rev. 9:21).

Blind to eternity, the secular mind thinks perpetual fair weather is an entitlement and scorns the truths of judgment, but its scorn can't rewrite history or reshape the universe. Wretched choices have wretched consequences, and man's choice in Eden exchanged the perfect world he instinctively desires for one of inevitable constraints. Darkened in understanding, he plods through it, defiantly rejecting God, certain he's invincible and immune to consequences. To sound calls to repentance, God restricts his freedom with things that disturb his circumstances, as symbolized by this vision's plagues. Nature's tsunamis, hurricanes and earthquakes prove man's mortality in a creation tainted by the fall! The rancid waters of worldly cisterns leave him thirsty! (Jer. 2:13). Bitterness and disillusionment emanate from his idols of wealth, sex and pride, and the course of human affairs confirms the darkness in his heart.

Defying the myth of progress, the past century was history's bloodiest—but still closed with a world blindly arguing right and wrong are only relative and the world's diversity should be celebrated. That diversity spawned Hitler, Stalin, Mao Tse Tung, Idi Amin, Mussolini, Saddam Hussein and scores of lesser tyrants. Their trail, strewn with more than 100 million corpses, left no cause for celebration. In spite of it, humanity still sees no need to repent of its murders, magic arts, immoralities or thefts.

God takes no delight in the death of the wicked (Ezek. 33:11), and heaven breaks its silence to warn them. Grace is the golden door to redemption, and God's trumpets prompt us to enter it while opportunity lasts. They repeat the moral lesson of Passover, urging us to choose between the yokes of heaven or hell. Unfortunately, their notes often fall on ears deafened by satanic deception. Wisdom cries out in the streets, but unbelief will not hear (Prov. 1:20-22). Like Pharaoh, it turns a deaf ear to God and readily dons the yoke of hell. In hardships, faith finds strength in God, but rebelliousness stiffens its resistance or hides behind a façade of denial.

Sin is invariably deceitful, enslaving and progressive. Those who persist in it are hardened by it. Not surprisingly, after this vision's attack by death's angels, callous survivors see no reason to repent. Perhaps, like our postmodern world, they think truth is unknowable and self is the only authority. The last two plagues of swarming locusts and angels of death offer a sobering commentary on the sinful nature's infinite gullibility and fatal consequences. Fields wasted by locusts never yield the intended crop. Those deceived by Satan's lies die never having known what it means to be fully alive.

Chapter 6

John's Fourth Vision—Faith in a Hostile World
Part 1: Witnessing

Then the angel I had seen standing on the sea and on the land raised his right hand to heaven. And he swore by him who lives for ever and ever, who created the heavens and all that is in them, the earth and all that is in it, and the sea and all that is in it, and said, "There will be no more delay!" (Rev. 10:5-6).

Recommended Reading:
Chapters 10 and 11 of Revelation

The prospect of six trumpets and plagues demonstrating humanity's fallen condition and exploitation by Satan is bleak, but <u>in a fallen order God also has a people</u>. John's fourth vision reveals them in four distinct scenes as witnesses in a hostile world, a woman separated from that world, the target of satanic beasts and a host standing triumphantly with the Lamb on Zion. <u>Each scene is a lesson on the life of faith</u>.

In the previous vision, six trumpets sounded. The seventh didn't, because the last trumpet is yet to sound. At the final service of Yom Kippur (Day of Atonement), a final trumpet signaled the end of the

time for repentance (Lev. 25:9). The life of the
Church is a time for repentance between the cross
and the day the last trumpet will sound. All four
scenes of John's vision define the interval as "*three
and one-half years*" (Rev. 12:14, NLV), otherwise
called "*1,260 days*" (Rev. 11:3;12:6) or "*a time, times
and half a time*" (Rev. 12:14) or "*forty-two months*"
(Rev. 11:2;13:5). Apocalyptic numbers are symbolic—not literal! "Seven," meaning completeness,
represents history from creation to the last judgment. The cross divides history in half, and the
interval between Calvary and the last trumpet sig-
naling Jesus' return is "three and one-half years."

To Jews, the number means oppression. In the
era between the testaments, Antiochus invaded
Jerusalem and desecrated the temple. It lay in dis-
grace for three and one-half years until its purifica-
tion—now commemorated by the Jewish festival of
Hanukah. John blends Jewish and Christian perspective to say believers will face satanic opposition
to their witness until the last trumpet sounds.[21]

In this vision, a mighty angel swearing by heaven
symbolizes an unbreakable oath. He warns of the day
when Jesus will suddenly return in power and
majesty to be glorified, close history, redeem His
people, separate sheep from goats and execute judgment. Until then, the Church is His witness on earth.

Go Witness! Go Measure!

*And when the seven thunders spoke, I was
about to write; but I heard a voice from heaven*

say, "Seal up what the seven thunders have
said and do not write it down.".…Then the voice
that I had heard from heaven spoke to me once
more: "Go, take the scroll that lies open in the
hand of the angel who is standing on the sea
and on the land" (Rev. 10:4,8).

I was given a reed like a measuring rod and was
told, "Go and measure the temple of God and the
altar, and count the worshipers there. But
exclude the outer court" (Rev. 11:1).

John listens to a voice like the sound of "*seven*
thunders" and begins to write; then another voice
from heaven stops him. The number seven signifies
completeness, and the ominous voice of seven thunders bespeaks a final verdict—but we cannot know
what it reveals. Tomorrow is a mystery known only
to God, and He calls us to witness to the world that
is rather than obsess over one that is to come.

The mighty angel with one foot on the land and
one foot on the sea, who tells John to "*take the scroll*"
and prophesy to many peoples, is the Lord Himself.
The Old Testament often refers to God as the "angel
of the Lord." When Abraham was about to slay his
son, an angel contradicted God's instruction and
stayed his hand (Gen. 22:15-18). Most commentators conclude the angel's voice was God's. An angel
visited Jacob saying; "*I am the God of Bethel*" (Gen.
31:13). At the burning bush, Moses saw the "*angel of*
the LORD" in the fire (Exod. 3:2), but its voice said;
"*I am the God of your father, the God of Abraham, the*

God of Isaac and the God of Jacob" (Exod. 3:6). David
disobediently took a census of Jerusalem. Afterward,
he saw the "*angel of the LORD*" with a sword drawn
over the city (1 Chron. 21:16) and pled for mercy,
saying, "*O LORD my God*" (1 Chron. 21:17).

John was a master of Old Testament Scripture
and describes the angel he sees with terms associated with deity. The angel is "*robed in a cloud*" (Rev.
10:1).Psalm 104 says God "*makes the clouds his
chariot*" (Ps. 104:3). Ezekiel speaks of His appear-
ance as "*a rainbow in the clouds*" (Ezek. 1:28). The
angel has a shout "*like the roar of a lion*" (Rev. 10:3).
Joel said, "*The LORD will roar from Zion*" (Joel 3:16).
And Amos said, "*The LORD roars from Zion*" (Amos
1:2). Hosea said of God, "*They shall walk after the
LORD: he shall roar like a lion*" (Hos. 11:10, KJV).
"*The voice of the LORD is over the waters; the God of
glory thunders,*" recalls Psalm 29:3.

The angel's command recalls Ezekiel (Rev. 10:9-
10). The prophet was called to eat a scroll that would
be both sweet and sour and then prophesy to a way-
ward Israel. God's Word, though sweet to the
prophet, included bitter judgment (Ezek. 3).
Similarly, some see the gospel as life while others see
it as death. Notably, the angel doesn't give John the
scroll. John has to take it (Rev. 10:8-10). Since John
was exiled, this call is implicitly to all Christians. As
God's witnesses, we're commanded to search the
Scriptures and actively "*take the scroll.*"

The angel also orders John to measure the
temple's inner court, or *naos*, with a reed (Rev. 11:1-
2). Mature reeds were often used for measurement

and grew up to nine feet.[22] The inner court was the place of holy sacrifice. Gentiles and casual observers could stroll in the outer court but dared not enter the inner one. That was a desecration worthy of death. Since the earthly temple no longer stood when John wrote, this measurement is not literal but spiritual. As a lesson in true witnessing, it contrasts those who offer themselves as living sacrifices to God with casual spectators wandering through His house.

The Power of the Gospel

Now when they have finished their testimony, the beast that comes up from the Abyss will attack them...But after the three and a half days a breath of life from God entered them, and they stood on their feet" (Rev. 11:7;11:11).

The vision combines paired images of lampstands, olive trees and witnesses facing the world's opposition and Satan's hatred. Some commentators label these paired images as the two testaments, the Word and the Spirit or the cross and the resurrection, but formulas based on "two" aren't essential to John's meaning. The prophecy of Zechariah linked witnesses, olive trees and lampstands as symbols of hope in the face of Israel's persecution and captivity. John faced persecution and captivity also, and he applies Zechariah's symbolism to describe the power of the gospel. As in the first vision, lampstands symbolize the Church (Rev. 11:4). Two witnesses symbolize certainty and authority (Rev. 11:3). In Jewish law, one witness couldn't convict,

but the word of two was deemed certain (Deut.
19:15). Olive trees symbolize holy anointing. Olive oil
was used exclusively to light the menorah and
anoint kings. Priests guarded it meticulously, as
described in the book of Numbers:

> *"Eleazar son of Aaron, the priest, is to have*
> *charge of the oil for the light, the fragrant*
> *incense, the regular grain offering and the*
> *anointing oil. He is to be in charge of the entire*
> *tabernacle and everything in it, including its*
> *holy furnishings and articles"* (Num. 4:16).

Lampstands, olive trees and witnesses form a
composite picture of the light of the gospel, anointed
by God and preached with undeniable certainty.

With unusual power, the witnesses close off the
sky to rain, turn waters to blood or bring plagues
(Rev. 11:6). Like the plagues in Egypt, the gospel is
God's call to repentance. When it's resisted, rain is
cut off and spiritual drought consigns the soul to a
thirsty land where waters that could have refreshed
become undrinkable blood.

Living in times of persecution, John sees Satan's
hatred of the gospel as a creature from the abyss
kills the witnesses in realms described as *"the great*
city, which is figuratively called Sodom and Egypt,
where also their Lord was crucified" (Rev. 11:8).
Some insist this is Jerusalem, but Jesus was crucified outside it. "Sodom" and "Egypt" more aptly
describe an unregenerate world.

Once dead, the witnesses are left unburied in the

streets—an act of supreme contempt in John's culture. A world in Satan's grip always holds the gospel in contempt and tries to leave it dead in the streets by shutting it out of every public forum, but truth doesn't go away just because the world denies it. Absolute truth will always exist, because God exists! His Word is never subject to a death sentence, and is never in jeopardy! No deception can erase it!

John sees God's witnesses revive with greater power after three and one-half days—a small portion of the Church's three and a half years—and the city that left them dead in the streets crumbles before them (Rev. 11:11-13). Persecution and martyrdom have limits. In the Church's earliest centuries, Rome succumbed to the power of the gospel after desperately trying to stamp it out. Later history has repeatedly proven the Church grows when persecuted. Truth will always revive, and ground that rejects it will fall before it.

The Glory of the Gospel

The seventh angel sounded his trumpet, and there were loud voices in heaven, which said, "The kingdom of the world has become the kingdom of our Lord and of his Christ and he will reign for ever and ever." Then God's temple in heaven was opened, and within his temple was seen the ark of his covenant. And there came flashes of lightning, rumblings, peals of thunder, an earthquake and a great hailstorm (Rev. 11:15,19).

John's blended images of thunder, lightning and the ark of the covenant draw on Israel's experience at Sinai and its temple to symbolize the power and glory of God. Thunder and lightning sounded when Moses received the law on tablets of stone (Exod. 20:18). Those sacred tablets, Aaron's rod and an urn with manna from the wilderness were kept in the ark of the covenant—a sacred relic engraved with gold and covered by a lid called the "mercy seat"—in the temple's Holy of Holies (Heb. 9:3-4). Its presence meant the glory of God was in the temple. It vanished when the first temple was destroyed in 586 BC and could not be located. Some said it would be found when the Messiah came. The meaning of a heavenly ark symbolizing the glory of God in an inner court is clear to John.

When Jesus' death severed the temple's veil (Matthew 27:51), the ark's resting place came into view. When He is crowned King of Kings and Lord of Lords, the heavenly ark of divine glory will appear (Rev. 11:19). Nature cried out in horror at Jesus' crucifixion, but it will cry out in awe at His coronation, and all will lie prostrate before Him.

The Vision in Perspective

"We give thanks to you, Lord God Almighty, the One who is and who was, because you have taken your great power and have begun to reign" (Rev. 11:17).

This scene's diverse images show the power and glory of the gospel. Pairs of lampstands, olive trees and witnesses symbolize a message that is anointed, definite and powerful. Until the seventh trumpet sounds and this world becomes the kingdom of our Lord, believers are God's witness, living to do His will in earth as it is in heaven. In a world filled with confusing voices, they're the voice of God to man and incite Satan's hatred. His attacks from the abyss may not seem as dramatic as John's imagery, but they're equally insidious. Knowing time is short and his fate is sealed, he tries to bury the gospel under lies, but it will survive his onslaughts.

If the angel's command to prophesy proves that true witnesses are called to proclaim the gospel, his command to measure proves they're also called to live it. The most powerful case for the gospel is the purity of those who profess it as they live under the control of the Holy Spirit. Power and purity can't be separated! With inspired insight, this scene links a powerful witness in the streets with the purity of the temple's inner court and the glory of its ark.

In that holy place, sacrifices were offered. Casual observers strolled outside it to satisfy maudlin curiosity but made no offerings. In the outer court, they were separated from the veil, the altar and the glory emanating from the ark. John takes no measure of them, because God takes no measure of nominal believers living only to entertain themselves. Certain they're rich, increased with goods and in need of nothing, they live by their own rules, thinking self is ultimate and life is an entitlement. They prize happiness above holiness and being blessed above being a blessing. They may admire the cross, but they never pick it up, and measuring them would be pointless!

The reed measuring true witnesses in the inner court is submission to God. To be a holy priesthood, we must offer ourselves as living sacrifices (Rom. 12:1). As we do, the Holy Spirit reveals the "*glory that excels*" (2 Cor. 3:10, NKJV) to us and through us. That is the meaning of this imagery. In Israel's temple, the ark of the covenant, symbolizing divine glory, rested in the inner court, signifying the law given to Moses. After receiving it, he was granted a partial glimpse of God's glory that transformed him with a heavenly radiance (Exod. 34:28-30). The glow on his face was a witness to Israel. Since he couldn't fully see the glory of God, the revelation was veiled. Symbolically, the temple's ark was forever behind a veil.

Calvary split the veil! God's temple is now the believing soul, and He dwells in the inner court of the heart. The transcendent glory that shone from Moses' face is no longer a presence from without but from within. It isn't symbolized in the coffer of an ornate ark but actualized in the redeemed soul. Someday, we'll stand triumphantly in the courts of heaven, bathed in a fuller revelation of it, but we have the foretaste here. By birth, we're inherently children of hell and know no glory but the vainglory of self-seeking. Grace introduces us to a glory that transcends and transforms. This scene tells us it will also triumph. We are witnesses to the transcendent, transforming and triumphant glory death can neither dim nor destroy! That's the message of John's diverse symbolism—and the majesty of our faith!

Chapter 7

John's Fourth Vision—Faith in a Hostile World

Part 2: In the World, but Not of It!

Now a great sign appeared in heaven: a woman clothed with the sun, with the moon under her feet, and on her head a garland of twelve stars (Rev. 12:1, NKJV).

Recommended Reading:
Chapter 12 of Revelation

In the second scene of God's people in the world, the image of a woman puts Satan's hatred for the gospel in perspective and proves God is faithful. Scriptural images of women often convey spiritual truths. Solomon's song refers to a faithful Israel as a bride. Hosea calls unfaithful Israel a harlot (Hos. 4:15, NKJV). In later visions, John adapts both images, calling the Church a bride (Rev. 19:7) and the world a harlot (Rev. 19:2, NKJV).

This scene introduces a woman, with the sun and moon beneath her feet, whose child would be caught up to the throne of God. The early Church scoured the Old Testament for its testimony to Jesus and saw Him as the *"Root of David,"* a conquering ruler and righteous judge identified in Psalm 89 as the seed of

a woman: "*His seed also I will make to endure forever,
And his throne as the days of heaven...It shall be
established forever like the moon, Even like the faithful
witness in the sky*" (Ps. 89:29,37, NKJV).

The woman John sees as a "*faithful witness in the
sky*" is a picture of the faithfulness of God. Our Lord,
born of woman, is the ultimate revelation of His faithfulness to man. Some mislabel this woman as Mary,
but Mary was human and this woman is a cosmic
presence. Some make her Israel, but she is virtuous
and for most of its history, Israel wasn't! Some call
her the Church, but this woman gives birth to the
"seed." The Church didn't give birth to Jesus. Later in
the vision, this "faithful witness in the sky" assumes
a second role as a faithful witness in the world's
wilderness (Rev. 12:6,17, NKJV). In that role, she is
the Church. God's people, sustained by His power,
are now the expression of His faithfulness.

The Dragon

> *And there was war in heaven. Michael and his
> angels fought against the dragon, and the
> dragon and his angels fought back. But he was
> not strong enough* (Rev. 12:7,8).

Putting the Church's warfare in perspective, John
sees Satan as a dragon trying to usurp God's throne
before time began. He is defeated and expelled.
Faithful angels celebrate as a loud voice responds:

> *"Now have come the salvation and the power
> and the kingdom of our God, and the authority*

of his Christ, For the accuser of our brothers,
who accuses them before our God day and
night, has been hurled down. They overcame
him by the blood of the Lamb and by the word
of their testimony" (Rev. 12:10,11).

This passage echoes Isaiah's description of Satan
as "Rahab," a pierced dragon hating righteousness
and all her children:

"Awake, awake! Clothe yourself with strength,
O arm of the LORD, awake, as in days gone
by, as in generations of old. Was it not you who
cut Rahab to pieces, who pierced that monster
through? Was it not you who dried up the sea,
the waters of the great deep?" (Isa. 51:9,10).

In Hebrew, *serpent* and *dragon* are the same
word. The serpent whose head would be bruised by
the seed of a woman (Gen. 3:15, NKJV) is the dragon
John sees trying to kill that seed at birth and failing
(Rev. 12:4-5). Some mistake this imagery for Herod's
attempt to kill Jesus at birth. In truth, the dragon
isn't Herod but Satan—the rebel! His hatred for God
began before time, and the rebel who failed in
heaven now attacks God's people on earth.

A Woman in the Wilderness

"Woe to the inhabitants of the earth and the sea!
For the devil has come down to you, having
great wrath, because he knows that he has a
short time." Now when the dragon saw that he

*had been cast to the earth, he persecuted the
woman who gave birth to the male Child But the
woman was given two wings of a great eagle,
that she might fly into the wilderness to her
place, where she is nourished for a time and
times and half a time, from the presence of the
serpent. So the serpent spewed water out of his
mouth like a flood after the woman, that he
might cause her to be carried away by the flood*
(Rev. 12:12-15, NKJV).

Having failed to capture God's throne, Satan's
covetousness turns to hatred for God's people. As a
slanderer and accuser whose time is short, the
eternal enemy of redemption desperately attacks the
Church. She may be his target, but she isn't a hap-
less victim retreating in terror. Her crown of twelve
stars—a reference to the twelve apostles—is the
stephanos worn by champion athletes in the ancient
Greek Olympics.

Her "wilderness" isn't a hiding place. God doesn't
call people to hide in remote communes but to shun
worldly values and priorities. Their wilderness is their
self-understanding as a people *in* the world but not *of*
it (John 17:13-18), and it's a place of great strength.
Just as Israel sojourned in the wilderness before
reaching the land of promise, believers are passing
through the world's wilderness en route to their final
home. But they're carried on eagles' wings—an Old
Testament symbol of deliverance echoing God's
words to Moses at Sinai: *"You yourselves have seen
what I did to Egypt, and how I carried you on eagles'*

wings and brought you to myself" (Exod. 19:4).

The prophet Isaiah also spoke of divine providence as eagles' wings:

> *Do you not know? Have you not heard?' The LORD is the everlasting God, the Creator of the ends of the earth. He will not grow tired or weary, and his understanding no one can fathom. He gives strength to the weary and increases the power of the weak. Even youths grow tired and weary, and young men stumble and fall; but those who hope in the LORD will renew their strength. They will soar on wings like eagles; they will run and not grow weary, they will walk and not be faint* (Isa. 40:28-31).

John's image of floods recalls Isaiah once again: "*When the enemy comes in like a flood, The Spirit of the LORD will lift up a standard against him*" (Isa. 59:19, NKJV).

Eagles are sent from heaven and floods are sent from hell, but both prove the faithfulness of God. Divine power, like eagles' wings, bears God's people above life's hills and valleys to breathe heaven's air. The earth swallows the satanic floodtides sweeping over contemporary culture in successive waves of materialism, hedonism, permissiveness, obscenity and violence, but God's people are secure under His standard.

The Vision in Perspective

Then the dragon was enraged at the woman and went off to make war against the rest of her offspring (Rev. 12:17).

This scene is an unapologetic call to holy separation from the world. Strange as it may seem to postmodernists deluded by a false sense of moral autonomy, Scripture consistently sees the world as Satan's kingdom of darkness and limits our choice to serving him or serving God. Our contemporary age has lost that perspective at great cost. As believers, we need to know our enemy. We don't wrestle against flesh and blood but against the prince of this world (Eph. 6:12), and his attacks define our rules of engagement. As a skilled tactician, his weapons of choice are floods, and their waters creep slowly but insidiously to ever more threatening levels. In today's culture, his tides of self-indulgence, moral decline, nominal religion and godless living have reached flood stage.

Those who succumb can't see who directs the waves lapping at their feet and confuse them for some inevitable process of change. What difference does it make if standards once held high have sunk from view? Lacking spiritual discernment, Satan's victims sense no foe and perceive no threat. Surely the waters that surround them are harmless! It's easy to relax and drift on the deepening tide. With pride as their only compass, they see conforming to the world as proof of intellectual maturity and congratulate themselves on their broadmindedness.

Confronted with choices, they no longer ask "Where's the holy?" but "Where's the harm?" and soon lower their standards further, from the permissible to the popular. Abdicating any redemptive role in the world, they let society set their agenda and join the dead bodies floating aimlessly downstream with every cultural current.

Only a live body can swim upstream, and true believers instinctively shun the lowlands sinking under satanic waters and seek higher ground. The path of least resistance is extremely broad, but it never leads there. Bethlehem's inn shunned the author and finisher of faith at His birth, and the world's priorities still exclude Him. His standards are alien to secular minds, and His cross is their reproach (Heb. 13:12-14, KJV). His true Church always lives out the contradiction of the cross. Like ancient Israel, it thrives when faithful to its calling to be a special people and fails whenever it becomes like the world around it.

Those who hunger and thirst for righteousness find it (Matt. 5:6), but they're always a voice in the world's wilderness! (Matt. 3:3, KJV). Saints and sinners aren't fellow travelers on a "faith journey." Their respective directions are diametrically opposite. Saints are in the world but not of it and would rather stand out than fit in, because their real home is heaven. In a world that denies the existence of sin, they speak of repentance. In a world blind to good and evil, they pursue holiness. In a world obsessed with self-esteem, they're selfless. In a world chasing pleasure, they follow after God. In a world of unguarded passions, their passion is the blood of the Lamb. In a world of deception, they're a testimony to integrity. Through the turmoil of time, their lives are a continuing testimony to the faithfulness of God.

Wearing victors' crowns, they make Christlikeness their ultimate goal and rise on wings of faith to heights where the air is pure and life's vistas are clear. Their wilderness isn't a place of confinement but a fortress armed by divine power. The unbounded horizons of God's love and grace seem like a wilderness to those who've never explored them, but saints know He is still the sovereign Creator. He is faithful to those who live by faith in Him—and His power can make wildernesses and solitary places spring forth and "*blossom as the rose*" (Isa. 35:1, NKJV)!

Chapter 8

John's Fourth Vision—Faith in a Hostile World
Part 3: Deadly Foes

Then I stood on the sand of the sea. And I saw a beast rising up out of the sea, having seven heads and ten horns, and on his horns ten crowns, and on his heads a blasphemous name...Then I saw another beast coming up out of the earth, and he had two horns like a lamb and spoke like a dragon (Rev. 13:1,11, NKJV).

Recommended Reading:
Chapter 13 of Revelation

After seeing God's people as a woman sheltered and separated in the wilderness, John sees the intensity of Satan's hatred as two hideous beasts enslave the world and kill the saints. In Scripture, beasts connote unclean things. The prophet Daniel described pagan empires in his day as a leopard, a bear and a lion (Dan. 7:4-6), but John's images are universal. The first beast has seven heads and ten horns. Each head is engraved with a blasphemous name. Unlike the victor's crown worn by the righteous woman earlier, each horn wears a crown of earthly authority. *Seven* shows completeness! *Ten* shows finality! This beast represents the corruption of

a world deifying material values and mocking everything holy. It's enthroned wherever vanity replaces the
worship of God with the worship of wealth, status or
power. John notes it suffered a near fatal wound (Rev.
13:3) when the serpent—source of its power—was
bruised at Calvary. It recovered to make war on
Christians. During the forty-two months or three and
one-half years of the Church's life (Rev. 13:5), both
beasts exult at centers of influence.

Seeing the world as a multiheaded beast with
blasphemous horns of power wouldn't require much
creativity from early Christians in the Roman
Empire. They weathered ruthless oppression in the
political sphere, suffering persecution, economic
deprivation and martyrdom under emperors like
Domitian—a tyrant who delegated power to equally
tyrannous local monarchs and governors.

Seeing the world as a satanically inspired beast
doesn't require much creativity now either. History
has anointed a succession of multiheaded beasts
waving alien standards over fleshly empires. At
times, their hostility to the godly has boiled over in
the death of martyrs—as in John's day. At other
times, it has taken subtler forms but still deceived
cultures and civilizations into blind submission.

The second beast, drawing authority from the
first and acting for it, is an indictment of false religion. The beast appears as a lamb but speaks as a
dragon. Its cloak of piety veils a satanic lie, and its
awesome power to deceive parodies Elijah—the
father of prophets—who called down fire from
heaven to convince the Israelites to choose between

God and idols (1 Kings 18:18-39). The idolatrous prophets of Baal couldn't duplicate his feat, but, with powerful deception, the second beast does (Rev. 13:13). It's well to remember truth isn't proven by outward signs but by God's Word.

John understood the beastly image of false religion very well. Throughout Rome's empire, idolatrous cults often forged unholy alliances with secular authorities and persecuted the early Church. For centuries since then, some have tried to pinpoint the beasts of John's vision by labeling Mohammed, Napoleon and all of the popes—to name a few—as their incarnation. Revelation's images and truths can't be reduced to a pinpoint. They're universal!

Secular priorities sway the world in every age, and spiritual counterfeits always walk hand in hand with them. Fallen humanity is still essentially religious, and Satan leads billions to give blind allegiance to gods of clay by worshiping ancestors, animals, trees and false prophets or chasing psychic experiences. He also parades as an angel of light (2 Cor. 11:14), seducing churches to prize relevance more than righteousness and social preferences more than sound doctrine. In the early twentieth century, he subverted many with insidious modernism, convincing them to dilute their message to reflect secular whims. As a result, today's liberal pulpits call down false fire to disavow the God of Scripture, deny the deity of His Son, reject the truth of His miracles, refuse the authority of His Word, preach only self-wrought salvation and breathe satanic benedictions over unrighteous causes. In our times, Satan subverts others with insidious post-modernism, seducing them to submit to secular whims, abandon a convicting message of salvation from sin, allow social convention to set their moral standards and measure success by popular appeal. When his ploy has come to fruition, its result will be equally disastrous!

Over the centuries, some have claimed these beasts portray the rule of an ultimately demonic figure called the antichrist. The Greek word *antichristos,* meaning "opposed to Christ," is found only in the letters of John the Apostle. Clarifying lurid speculation in his day, he said many spirits of antichrist were already in the world, denying Jesus' lordship (1 John 2:18; 2 John 1:7). Paul spoke of a *"man of lawlessness"* deceiving and blaspheming (2 Thess. 2:3-12). Many combine these Scriptures and conclude a future "antichrist" will arise to be judged and destroyed at the Lord's return.

Undeniably, Paul saw accelerated deterioration prior to Jesus' return. God would judge a world fallen away from faith, rebellious towards all things godly and ruled by a *"man of lawlessness."* Perhaps he envisioned a single corrupt individual holding all power. Perhaps he saw mankind in a heightened state of rebellion or simply a rotting world system. Scholars debate these variables, but their conjecture is inconclusive. Speculating about future tyrants serves no purpose. Two thousand years have passed since John and Paul said spirits of antichrist and lawlessness were already present. Therefore, these spirits must be trans-temporal and present in every age!

The prospect of an unclean world captive to satanic deception, blaspheming God and hostile to saintliness is not something we must wait until history's close to see. It's all around us, mocking holiness and denying the existence of any binding moral law. During the figurative three and one-half years of its life, the Church always faces the beasts of secular values and false religion. They aren't in the wings but in the streets, making war on the saints in every age!

The world and true faith are always at odds, as proven by their responses to the beasts. Christians see the beasts as evil personified. The world loves them! What appalls the godly enthralls the ungodly. As masters of deception, the false beasts of worthless values and worthless religion are embraced by a world eternally alien to the cross and enamored with lust, fleshliness and pride. Seeing no immunity to persecution or suffering, John calls believers to patience and faith. God will judge the wicked.

> *If anyone has an ear, let him hear. He who leads into captivity shall go into captivity; he who kills with the sword must be killed with the sword. Here is the patience and faith of the saints (Rev. 13:9,10, NKJV).*

Marks and Numbers

> *He causes all, both small and great, rich and poor, free and slave, to receive a mark on their right hand or on their foreheads, and that no one may buy or sell except the one who has the*

mark of the name of the beast, or the number of his name. Here is wisdom. Let him who has understanding calculate the number of the beast, for it is the number of a man: His number is 666 (Rev. 13:16-18, NKJV).

Historicists claim this scene's imagery of beastly marks is a veiled reference to Christians being barred from marketplaces where Roman coinage deified Caesar. That view reduces the scene to a comment on trade and commerce in John's day rather than the symbolic "three and one-half years" of the Church's existence. Revelation isn't simply a mirror of ancient history. Futurists claim a future antichrist will implant computer chips under the skin or visibly mark people to show his ownership. Sinners needn't be etched with marks to show whose service they're in! Their priorities are already self-evident.

John's "mark of the beast" recalls Moses' comment on Passover observance: "*This observance will be for you like a sign on your hand and a reminder on your forehead that the law of the LORD is to be on your lips*" (Exod. 13:9).

The hand symbolizes man's actions and the forehead his thoughts. The "mark" of Passover meant the Israelites' actions and thoughts would glorify God. The beastly mark is carnality and subservience to the flesh. Its antithesis is the "marks of Christ."

Many have tried to interpret the number 666 through an ancient Jewish formula that ascribed numerical values to alphabetic letters. They've labeled many historic figures as this vision's beasts by assigning corresponding numerical values to each letter of their names to arrive at a sum of 666. As early as Irenaeus in AD 168, ancients gave up such exercises as a lost cause. If John was making a coded reference to a ruler of his day, the code is buried with him.

More likely, John's number reflects rabbinical thought where the number six is the number of man created on the sixth day. (The original text of Revelation refers to "man"—not to "a man.") The rabbis said the first six days of creation each had a morning and evening but the seventh had no evening since man was intended for an everlasting fellowship on which the sun would never set. His fall set him back to the sixth day. Intended for endless fellowship with God, he's living in a lesser condition. Life was intended to be a seven—the number of completeness! Instead it's a six! John repeats the number three times to emphasize man's bleak subservience to an unholy trinity of fallen nature, worldly values and worthless religions.

The Vision in Perspective

This calls for patient endurance and faithfulness on the part of the saints (Rev. 13:10).

Infatuation with the world is enmity towards God, and John sees it personified in a terrifying image of satanic beasts emanating from the depths of hell, deceiving the world into submission and slaughtering everything holy. They form a vile portrait so shocking that many recoil and assume they're a dark specter of the future. With infinite naiveté, people speak in awe of a future three and a half years when Satan will dispatch some tyrant to place his mark on the earth.

If Satan's mark is yet to be seen, whose mark has scarred recorded history since the fall in Eden? Who deceives the multitudes worshiping leaders who preach salvation in their own names and spend trillions on arms and weaponry while billions starve? Who makes wealth and influence masters of all political systems and self-interest the rationale behind every economic theory? Who makes idols of entertainers and messiahs of those who manage money or power skillfully? Who promotes the holocaust of abortions, drug addiction, aids, terrorism, pornography, crime, perversion, divorce, wars, suicide bombings and all the other infinitely vile elements in our world's panorama?

Whose second beast of false religion rises to proclaim a myriad of false gospels more likely to indulge pride and self-righteousness than to dethrone them? Who's the author and finisher of the faiths professed by blasphemous cults or legions of idolaters? Who tempts the Church to replace "Thus Saith the Lord!" with "Thus Saith Man!" and embrace worldly values and live for the sixes of time rather than the sevens of eternity?

The beasts are the personification of carnality and the pseudo piety that leaves it enthroned, and their most terrifying attribute isn't their power to kill but their power to deceive. Martyrdom can't destroy faith, but the deceptions of secular values and false doctrines are lethal threats. What is more deadly than the enemy who operates in complete stealth? Satan's signature would be easily spotted if it were just Caesar's likeness on a Roman coin or a computer chip under the skin, but he's far more cunning. As the master deceiver, he moves unseen through the corridors of society, enslaving and damning his followers. The self-seeking kneel at his altars and swear allegiance. Publicly branding them would be redundant! Satan already owns the thoughts and deeds of those who live solely for designer labels, prestigious addresses, exotic cars, worldly status and membership in the right country clubs, Quiet conformity to fleshly values imprints his indelible mark on their souls imperceptibly and painlessly.

The shock value of John's imagery makes us wonder if our consecration could withstand an ultimate test. Blind to the real urgency of the question, we create an imaginative fiction about future tyrants. Why? The beasts of secular values and false doctrine are already within the gates, testing the integrity of our motives and the allegiance of our hearts every day. As masters of deception, they operate in great stealth, taking the measure of human pride and using it to forge chains that enslave. Their victims reduce life to a contest with their peers and live to glorify themselves rather than God.

Truth is the impenetrable armor against that deception, but can it be found in our inward parts? Are we saints living by patience and faith or sinners living by pride and presumption? Whose word masters our thinking? Whose values set our priorities? Is our quest for status and recognition more urgent than our quest for holiness? Do we glory more in financial assets and material possessions than in God? Do we prize the world's pleasures more than service and its acclaim more than sacrifice? What cross do we carry in Jesus' name? Those who live for the world wear the beast's mark. Whose marks can be seen in the deeds of our hands and the direction of our hearts?

Chapter 9

John's Fourth Vision—Faith in a Hostile World

Part 4: On the Mountaintop

And they sang a new song before the throne and before the four living creatures and the elders. No one could learn the song except the 144,000 who had been redeemed from the earth. These are those who did not defile themselves with women, for they kept themselves pure. They follow the Lamb wherever he goes. They were purchased from among men and offered as firstfruits to God and the Lamb. No lie was found in their mouths; they are blameless (Rev. 14:3-5).

Recommended Reading:
Chapter 14 of Revelation

In three scenes of this vision, John saw God's people as witnesses scorned by society, as a people in the world but not of it and as the target of Satan's hatred. Each scene was a call to vigilance and consecration. Fortunately, the people of God do not stand in their own strength. In the fourth and final scene, he sees a redeemed host of 144,000 standing in triumph with the Lamb on Mt. Zion.

Jews revered Mt. Zion as King David's burial place. As Jerusalem's highest point, it was a natural bulwark symbolizing strength, and its name became a synonym for the highest place spiritually. Micah extolled it:

> *In the last days the mountain of the LORD's temple shall be established as chief among the mountains; it will be raised above the hills, and peoples will stream to it. Many nations will come and say, "Come, let us go up to the mountain of the LORD, to the house of the God of Jacob. He will teach us his ways, so that we may walk in his paths." The law will go out from Zion, the word of the LORD from Jerusalem* (Micah 4:1,2).

In New Testament times, the palace of Herod the Great—later to become Pilate's residence—stood on Mt. Zion. Pilate, awakened the night of Jesus' arrest, probably first interrogated Him there. Some early Christians claimed the upper room at Pentecost was on Mt. Zion and still saw it as a symbol of the highest place spiritually. The author of Hebrews likened redemption to "*Mount Zion and to the city of the living God, the heavenly Jerusalem, to an innumerable company of angels, to the general assembly and church of the firstborn*" (Heb. 12:22-23 NKJV).

This scene implicitly contrasts Mt. Zion and Mt. Sinai through images from Judaism's second pilgrimage festival known to Christians as Pentecost and to Jews as the Feast of Weeks or Shavu'ot. As ordained by God, it was held seven weeks after Passover at harvest time to commemorate the covenant at Sinai: "*Six days you shall labor, but on the seventh day you shall rest; even during the plowing season and harvest you must rest. Celebrate the Feast of Weeks with the firstfruits of the wheat harvest*" (Exod. 34:21,22).

At Passover, God delivered the Jews from Egypt! At Sinai, He chose them as a covenant people. They regard Sinai as the true measure of their freedom, confirming the reason for their deliverance. The phrase "standing at Sinai" is common parlance among Jews, signifying their covenant obligations. That covenant anticipated fulfillment when they would build the temple of God on Mt. Zion in Jerusalem, "*Beautiful for situation, the joy of the whole earth*" (Ps. 48:2, KJV). Some Jewish spiritual disciplines are called *aliyah*, which means growing in the knowledge of God.[23] Since Zion was a high point, one had to ascend it. Physical ascent became a synonym for spiritual ascent or *aliyah*, as echoed by the psalmist: "*Who may ascend the hill of the LORD? Who may stand in his holy place? He who has clean hands and a pure heart, who does not lift up his soul to an idol or swear by what is false*" (Ps. 24:3). Sinai's promise was conditional upon Israel keeping God's commands and walking in His statutes (Lev. 26). Israel failed!

Jesus' death initiated a new covenant for the world (Luke 22:20), and Mt. Zion represents the full-ness He purchased on the cross. At Sinai, God's laws were written in stone. At Zion, the Holy Spirit writes them in the heart (2 Corinthians 3:3-6). Sinai was in the wilderness because it was only a promise. Zion is fulfillment, and Christians are the promised household of faith (Gal. 6:10, NKJV), standing in the holy place. In an earlier vision, they stood before God. This time, they stand with Him.

Scripture never makes Jesus' lordship a discretionary option, and in this vision believers follow Him wherever He goes (Rev. 14:4). Unlike the world wearing the marks of the beast, they wear the marks of godliness. John describes them as *"firstfruits"* offered to God and virgins undefiled with women (Rev. 14:4). At Shavu'ot, the harvest's first fruits were offered to God free of blemish (Exod. 23:19). "Virgins" symbolize purity! Our Lord wills to present a pure Church to God, free of spot or blemish. Christlike character is also transparently honest. Peter described Jesus as One who *"committed no sin, and no deceit was found in his mouth"* (1 Peter 2:22). The psalmist said those who ascend the holy hill haven't *"sworn deceitfully"* (Ps. 24:4 NKJV) and later repeated the theme: *"Blessed is the man whose sin the LORD does not count against him and in whose spirit there is no deceit"* (Ps. 32:2). Isaiah said of the Messiah: *"He was assigned a grave with the wicked, and with the rich in his death, though he had done no violence, nor was any deceit in his mouth"* (Isa. 53:9).

When God gave the law at Sinai, thunder accompanied His voice and the people dared not approach the mountain for fear (Exod. 20:18). At Zion, the Lamb speaks and thunder sounds, but it's musical, and heaven's harps echo through it (Rev. 14:2). To commemorate Sinai, each year Jews sing words from Psalm 30:2: *"O LORD my God, I called to you for help and you healed me."*

The new song of redemption only the followers of the Lamb can sing is the voice of the indwelling Spirit of God interceding. Their music replaces the language of deceit.

To a first-century reader, the lofty image of Mt. Zion must have seemed unreal in a world of persecution and martyrdom. Putting the death of martyrs in perspective, a voice from heaven commands John to write of those who die in the Lord and rest from their labors. *"Then I heard a voice from heaven say, 'Write: Blessed are the dead who die in the Lord...' 'Yes,' says the Spirit, 'they will rest from their labor, for their deeds will follow them'"* (Rev. 14:13).

To live under the Lamb is to dwell on Zion, and to die is gain (Phil. 1:21). The saint's rest is not a time out or a vacation. It's the distinction crowning outstanding achievement like the prize won after completing a marathon or the medal given after a worthy mission. The lives of the righteous are a benediction, and their death is a reward.

Babylon's Doom

"Fallen! Fallen is Babylon the Great, which made all the nations drink the maddening wine of her adulteries" (Rev. 14:8).

As the vision progresses, angels flying in midair warn of Babylon's doom and call the people to worship and glorify God. Zion symbolizes redemption! Babylon symbolizes judgment! During the era of the prophets, it was Israel's major foe. It invaded and led Israel into seventy years of captivity. Jeremiah foresaw the event but also saw Babylon's fall and said:

> *"Flee from Babylon! Run for your lives! Do not be destroyed because of her sins. It is time for the LORD's vengeance; he will repay her what she deserves. Babylon was a gold cup in the LORD's hand; she made the whole earth drunk. The nations drank her wine; therefore they have now gone mad. Babylon will suddenly fall and be broken"* (Jer. 51:6-8).

John saw Rome as another Babylon in his day but, regardless of geography or history, he knew a corrupt world would be judged. Rotting structures are certain to collapse. His language echoes the psalmist: *"For in the hand of the LORD there is a cup, And the wine is red; It is fully mixed, and He pours it out; Surely its dregs shall all the wicked of the earth Drain and drink down"* (Ps. 75:8, NKJV).

In this vision, Babylon is the fleshliness of the world, and this scene's Shavu'ot harvest theme reflects its doom. Jews believed agricultural harvests reflected God's sovereignty, because His law was the eternal, immutable Word that created the universe and bound all of nature—not just human behavior. Obedience meant blessing and a good harvest! Disobedience meant suffering and a bad harvest! The judgment of Babylon shows moral accountability in the light of a bitter final harvest.

John likens dying in Babylon to harvesting grapes of wrath (Rev. 14:10) and makes their wine a sea of blood as wide as Israel's boundaries—originally deemed to be 1,600 furlongs. The number 1,600 also implies 4 corners of earth multiplied 4 times and then by 10 x 10. The meaning is clear! Death's sweep is universal, and its angels leave no one untouched. Babylon offers no protection. The only refuge is with death's conqueror on Zion!

The Vision in Perspective

No one could learn the song except the 144,000 who had been redeemed from the earth (Rev. 14:3).

This scene contrasts images of Zion and Babylon to make a statement about triumphant faith. In a world fundamentally hostile to righteousness, the people of God follow the Lamb wherever He goes and stand secure on Zion while the citizens of Babylon, benighted by their own vanity, face hopeless death and a lost eternity. Importantly, faith's triumph doesn't depend on Babylon's doom—which this vision only foresees. Faith needn't destroy the world to overcome it. The Lamb has already prevailed!

A second contrast between Zion and Sinai is subtler but celebrates the high calling and privilege of the Lamb's followers. For Jews, Sinai was a loving bond between God and Israel, and the Shavu'ot festival often cites a poem written by Rabbi Meir ben Isaac of Worms in the 11th century and later adapted for a familiar gospel song:

Could we with ink the ocean fill, were the sky of parchment made,

Were every stalk on earth a quill and every man a scribe by trade,

To write the love of God above would drain the ocean dry,

Nor could the scroll contain the whole though stretched from sky to sky.

If the scroll at Sinai was a bond of love, how much richer is the bond represented by Zion? At Sinai, God spoke from the mountain none dared approach and wrote His laws in stone. On Zion, He is the Lamb who writes His love in blood and His law on the human heart. At Sinai, God was on the mountain alone. At Zion, the Lord stands with His people. Sinai meant obedience to the divine. Zion means complete ownership by the divine, and the music echoing from it is a sweet song of redemption. It wasn't written in tempests of fire and smoke but by the power of the resurrection, and its beauty holds angels in awe. At Sinai, God spoke to man. At Zion, He speaks from within him—indwelling him in a relationship so intimate the breath of the Spirit of God intercedes for him, and His voice interceding is the new song only the redeemed can sing (Rev. 14:3).

God faithfully leads faithful people to higher ground. They don't dwell beneath Sinai shrouded in clouds but on Zion—and that's the true measure of their freedom! Their spiritual habitation isn't a place of heavy crosses and unbearable burdens. It's a narrow path that follows the Lamb wherever He goes, but His steps lead invariably to the mountain's summit. That place of pure fellowship with Him is an unassailable fortress! As the psalmist once said: *"Those who trust in the LORD are like Mount Zion, which cannot be shaken but endures forever"* (Ps. 125:1).

Chapter 10

John's Fifth Vision—
Seven Plagues, One Judgment

I saw in heaven another great and marvelous sign: seven angels with the seven last plagues—last, because with them God's wrath is completed (Rev. 15:1).

Then I heard a loud voice from the temple saying to the seven angels, "Go pour out the seven bowls of God's wrath on the earth" (Rev. 16:1).

Recommended Reading:
Chapters 15 and 16 of Revelation

The believer's mission will end when Jesus returns to judge the world, and John sees the last judgment as seven plagues. In a previous vision, trumpet calls to repentance preceded each plague. This time, no trumpets sound! Suddenly and without warning, seven "angels of the Presence," adorned with golden sashes, simultaneously pour out all the bowls of divine wrath in one decisive event.

Judgment condemns evil, but it also vindicates righteousness, and John hears angels accompanied by heaven's harps sing a new *"song of Moses...and the song of the Lamb"* (Rev. 15:3).The first "song of Moses" celebrated Israel's deliverance at the Red Sea and spoke of banishing the ungodly kingdoms of Edom, Philistia and Moab:

*"In your unfailing love you will lead the people
you have redeemed. In your strength you will
guide them to your holy dwelling. The nations
will hear and tremble; anguish will grip the
people of Philistia. The chiefs of Edom will be
terrified, the leaders of Moab will be seized
with trembling, the people of Canaan will melt
away; terror and dread will fall upon them. By
the power of your arm they will be as still as
stone—until your people pass by, Oh LORD,
until the people you bought pass by. You will
bring them in and plant them on the mountain
of your inheritance—the place, O LORD, You
made for Your dwelling, that sanctuary O Lord,
Your hands established. The LORD will reign
for ever and ever"* (Exod. 15:13-18).

The new *"song of Moses...and the song of the
Lamb"* is a song of praise heralding God's judgment on
unrighteousness. It begins with: *"Great and marvelous
are Your works, Lord God Almighty!"* (Rev. 15:3,
NKJV). Those words echo Psalm 92, sung on Jewish
Sabbaths and celebrating God's triumph when *"all the
workers of iniquity shall be scattered"* (Ps. 92:9,
NKJV), with these words: *"How great are your works,
O LORD, how profound your thoughts!"* (Ps. 92:5).

This imagery tells us God's purpose in creation
was fellowship with man, and He will vindicate it by
leading His people in a second exodus to their
eternal home. The image is balanced by the fearful
prospect of divine judgment on the ungodly, symbolized by plagues.

Fleshly Corruption

The first angel went and poured out his bowl on the land, and ugly and painful sores broke out on the people (Rev. 16:2).

This vision's plagues parallel the phases of a criminal trial, beginning with the evidence for a conviction as the first bowl reveals ugly, painful sores on worshipers of the beast. In Greek, sores are *helkos*—or open wounds. Isaiah spoke of sores as the mark of ungodliness: "*Your whole head is injured, your whole heart afflicted. From the sole of your foot to the top of your head there is no soundness—only wounds and welts and open sores*" (Isa. 1:5,6).

The last judgment will expose the wretchedness of sin. Paul warned the that Galatians sowing to the flesh would reap corruption (Gal. 6:8, NKJV), and James' general epistle was similarly direct: "*Your gold and silver are corroded. Their corrosion will testify against you and eat your flesh like fire*" (Jas. 5:3).

Blood and Water

The second angel poured out his bowl on the sea, and it turned into blood like that of a dead man, and every living thing in the sea died. The third angel poured out his bowl on the rivers and springs of water, and they became blood (Rev. 16:3,4).

Judgment means accountability, here symbolized as angels pour out the second and third bowls, turning rivers and the sea to blood and permeating the world with a suffocating stench. In arid middle-eastern lands, water was scarce and highly prized, and Scripture often makes it a synonym for the life-giving grace of God. Jesus described the work of the Holy Spirit as "*rivers of living water*" (John 7:38, NKJV) and told the Samaritan woman "*living water*" would be a "*a spring of water welling up*" within (John 4:10-14). Repentance is sometimes presented as an invitation to drink life-giving water. Today, we can repent and draw joyfully from the wells of salvation. When our Lord appears to judge the world, life-giving water will no longer flow. On that day of accountability, time for repentance will be gone. Life-giving water will turn to blood as a symbol of death replaces a symbol of life.

Searing Light and Infinite Darkness

The fourth angel poured out his bowl on the sun, and the sun was given power to scorch people with fire. They were seared by the intense heat and they cursed the name of God, who had control over these plagues, but they refused to repent and glorify him. The fifth angel poured out his bowl on the throne of the beast, and his kingdom was plunged into darkness (Rev. 16:8-10).

Judgment includes a verdict and a sentence. The fourth and fifth plagues show these through the images of light and darkness. In the fourth, the sun's light becomes a scorching blaze. Attacked by his source of warmth and comfort, man curses God. Tragically, the gospel's light that can warm cold hearts and light dark lives will become scorching fire at the last judgment. Rebels, feeling its verdict, will blaspheme God.

The fifth plague shows a lost eternity through the symbolism of darkness—a term frequently used in Scripture to describe spiritual death or eternal damnation. Jesus Himself gave two parables—one about a wedding banquet and another about unprofitable servants—and said those not wearing proper garments for the banquet and worthless servants would be "*cast...into...outer darkness*" (Matt. 22:13;25:30, NKJV). "*God is light; in him there is no darkness at all*" (1 John 1:5). To be forever removed from His presence is to be left groping blindly.

A Parched Riverbed, Frogs and Hail

The sixth angel poured out his bowl on the great river Euphrates, and its water was dried up...Then I saw three evil spirits that looked like frogs; they came out of the mouth of the dragon, out of the mouth of the beast and out of the mouth of the false prophet. They are spirits of demons performing miraculous signs, and they go out to the kings of the whole world, to gather them for the battle on the great day of God Almighty...From the sky huge hailstones of about a hundred pounds each fell upon men (Rev. 16:12,14,21).

The last judgment will doom unrighteousness universally. To symbolize that, the final plagues include an intriguing image of the Euphrates River drying up. It was a defensive bulwark in the time of Solomon and formed Israel's primary defense. The symbolism of it drying up means all defense is gone.

Sin's deceitful facades will crumble at the last judgment. Satan loves darkness and deception, but the One in whom there is no darkness says of Himself: "*I AM THAT I AM*" (Exod. 3:14, KJV). He needs no façade, and He hates them. His final judgment will reveal the thoughts, deeds and intents of human hearts and expose spiritual nakedness.

Recalling the nuisance plague of frogs that befell Egypt, John mocks Satan's demons, false prophets and lying spirits as pathetic frogs marshaling in defiance at Megiddo after their river has gone dry. Just as the Euphrates is a synonym for boundaries, Megiddo is a synonym for battle. Many were fought there, but this one is spiritual—not literal. In any case, it's a non-event! The frogs' resistance instantly evaporates! Just as light vanquishes darkness and sound banishes silence, our Lord's appearing will make truth plain and crush all lies.

Following a final and decisive earthquake, John sees great hailstones raining down on Babylon. This image of ultimate destruction would be as familiar in the first century as a mushroom cloud is in ours. Rome leveled Jerusalem with catapults, launching rocks weighing up to 100 pounds. Pompeii was buried under a catastrophic volcano. This imagery shows Satan's kingdom irreversibly leveled and destroyed.

Sensationalists conjure calamitous battles over earthly stakes to explain these scenes, but their view diminishes God and exalts His foes unworthily. The One who can bid mountains and isles to flee needn't battle armies of pathetic frogs to establish His authority. Satan will make no final stand. His fate was determined at Calvary, and his only prospect is a final fall!

The Vision in Perspective

"Behold, I come like a thief! Blessed is he who stays awake" (Rev. 16:15).

Nothing is less fashionable than the theme of judgment! We adamantly foreclose extraneous measurements as unreasonable intrusions on our personhood. Lazing idly in the morass of relative standards, moral imprecision and bizarre notions of truth being something we will for ourselves, we reject demands and rules and want only self-affirmation. Surely our slumber should not be disturbed! Recalling the parable of foolish virgins sleeping before a bridegroom's appearing (Matt. 25:1-13), John hears the words, *"Blessed is he who stays awake"* and sees a sobering panorama of instantaneous judgment.

Whether postmodern thinkers like it or not, sin offends a holy God and will ultimately fill the bowls of His wrath. At a date known only to Him, He will pour them out. Peter warned of a single *"day of the Lord"* when Jesus will appear as history's judge with unchallengeable power to suddenly lay the earth bare:

*But the day of the Lord will come like a thief.
The heavens will disappear with a roar; the
elements will be destroyed by fire, and the
earth and everything in it will be laid
bare...That day will bring about the destruction of the heavens by fire, and the elements
will melt in the heat. But in keeping with his
promise we are looking forward to a new
heaven and a new earth, the home of righteousness* (2 Pet. 3:10-13).

At creation, the words "*Let there be light*" (Gen.
1:3) ignited billions of stars to fuel the energy of the
universe. The voice that spoke creation into existence with those four words will someday dismantle
it with three: "*It is done!*" (Rev. 16:17). On that day,
He'll judge the thoughts, deeds and intents of the
heart. Greed, lust and pride will become repulsive
sores. Status and position will mock those who live
for them. The gospel's light will be a searing blaze for
the ungodly, and pomp and presumption, stripped of
their facades, will face the ultimate dark night of the
soul. False prophets and deceivers will perish as
every manifestation of evil is judged.

When God spoke at Sinai, thunder sounded (Exod.
20:18). John hears thunder and feels quakes as
Babylon—embodiment of a sinful world—is vanquished
as islands and mountains flee away (Rev. 16:18).

Despite that ominous prospect, John also sees the
beauty of redemption. At Passover, Pharaoh's forces
were suddenly engulfed while the Israelites escaped
and celebrated deliverance with their "*song of Moses.*"

After crossing the Red Sea, they received the covenant of law and set up a tabernacle in the wilderness. Their story, as recorded in Exodus, ended as God's glory filled the place of worship (Exod. 40:34).

John sees the parallel. Israel was delivered from Pharaoh, and Christians have been freed from the slavery of sin. Today they're passing through the world's wilderness en route to the land of promise. The Lord's appearing in power and great glory will complete their exodus from earth's arid wastes and unforgiving valleys. On a great and final day, they'll forever forsake its corrupt arena to gather in heaven's temple in an endless celebration of deliverance, singing a new *"song of Moses...and the song of the Lamb"* (Rev. 15:3) as they're truly planted in the mountain of their inheritance—the sanctuary the Lord has established (Exod. 15:17). His glory will fill it as they join heavenly choirs in an everlasting song of praise: *"Great and marvelous are your deeds, Lord God Almighty. Just and true are your ways, King of the ages. Who will not fear you, O Lord, and bring glory to your name? For you alone are holy"* (Rev. 15:3,4).

Chapter 11

John's Sixth Vision—The Harlot and the Bride

"Come, I will show you the punishment of the great prostitute, who sits on many waters. With her the kings of the earth committed adultery and the inhabitants of the earth were intoxicated with the wine of her adulteries" (Rev. 17:1,2).

Recommended Reading:
Revelation 17:1 to 19:10

In this vision, John sees another aspect of the world's judgment in the image of a pompous prostitute named after Babylon. The city's association with vanity was exemplified in the tower of Babel, where man tried to reach heaven and deify himself. Its identification with harlotry goes back to its founder, Nimrod—a figure from the book of Genesis (Gen. 10:8-12) whose wife was exceedingly beautiful and notoriously promiscuous. In ancient times, many idolatrous fertility cults made her a symbol of worship.

In the prophetic era, Babylon was Israel's major foe, and the Old Testament names it more than any city except Jerusalem. Jeremiah pled with Israel to resist Babylon's seductions, turn from idols and trust solely in God:

> *"Flee from Babylon! Run for your lives! Do not be destroyed because of her sins. It is time for the LORD's vengeance; he will repay her what she deserves. Babylon was a gold cup in the LORD's hand; she made the whole earth drunk. The nations drank her wine; therefore they have now gone mad. Babylon will suddenly fall and be broken"* (Jer. 51:6-8).

His pleas were ignored, and Babylon led Israel into seventy years of ignominious captivity. The prophet knew a holy God would ultimately judge the evil city. A few generations later, it perished as a world empire.

In John's day, pagan Rome was another Babylon controlling the world from the British Isles to central Africa. Reigning with legendary decadence, it was truly a harlot, personifying all blasphemies, adorned by fabulous wealth, sitting on *"many waters,"* committing immorality with kings and intoxicating earth's inhabitants with her seductions. Its obscene wealth probably accounted for about 90 percent of all global resources, and its ruthlessness matched its wealth! With callous brutality, its empire ran on the backs of slaves from subjugated nations.

Just as ancient Babylon persecuted Israel, Rome tyrannized the Church. John calls Babylon *"the great city that rules over the kings of the earth"* but wisely doesn't name Rome specifically. Doing so might have been fatal. His language reflects his world, but his point is the lesson to be drawn from Babylon's destruction. This *"MOTHER OF HARLOTS"* (Rev. 17:5, NKJV) is the moral rot of a corrupted world *"drunk* with the blood of the saints and with the blood of the martyrs" (Rev. 17:6, NKJV). John warns of her guile and pleads with the faithful to come out of her. "*Come out of her, my people, so that you will not share in her sins, so that you will not receive any of her plagues; for her sins are piled up to heaven, and God has remembered her crimes*" (Rev. 18:4,5).

Jeremiah referred to ancient Babylon's "*gold cup*" of fleshly enticements making all the earth drunk. John's description of the spiritual Babylon is more vivid: "*The woman was dressed in purple and scarlet, and was glittering with gold, precious stones and pearls. She held a golden cup in her hand, filled with abominable things and the filth of her adulteries*" (Rev. 17:4).

Her abominations are fleshly arrogance, and the beast she rides to destruction is Satan, who carries temptation across the earth. She is also called "*MYSTERY*" (Rev. 17:5). Many pagan religions are mystery religions, but this title has deeper meaning. Fleshly desire is deceitfully enticing and always hides Satan's agenda. As a master deceiver, he never discloses the full weight of sin's consequences and artfully leads the world to dismiss his existence. When he's revealed at the judgment, it will be shocked to see him (Rev. 17:8).

Seven Kings and Ten Rulers

This calls for a mind with wisdom. The seven heads are seven hills on which the woman sits. They are also seven kings. Five have fallen, one is, the other has not yet come; but

*when he does come, he must remain for a
little while (Rev. 17:9,10).*

Seven means completeness, and this vision's
seven kings depict all history. Five are gone, a sixth
rules in John's day and a seventh and final "king" will
surface at the last judgment. Those who make
Revelation a set of secret codes contrive "This is that!"
formulas to explain these kings. Historicists make
Babylon a pseudonym for ancient Jerusalem or Rome.
Those favoring Jerusalem insist John wrote before it
fell in AD 70 and before Rome persecuted Christians,
but their view doesn't explain his exile. Most favor
Rome and label emperors from a list including Julius,
Augustus, Tiberius, Gaius, Claudius, Caligula, Nero,
Vespasian and Domitian as this vision's rulers.

For centuries, futurists made the kings into
empires and selectively listed five pre-New Testament
empires, labeling the sixth as Rome. Invariably they
concluded the seventh was a future entity and, over
the years, labeled all of the papal succession, many
medieval kingdoms or empires and, in the twentieth
century, the League of Nations, the Third Reich, the
Soviet Union, the United Nations, the Club of Rome,
the G7 group and the European Common Market—to
mention a few—as its incarnation.

Apocalyptic symbols reveal principles and truths—
not future events. Using them to conjure "end times"
fantasies around earthly institutions misses their
point. Babylon is neither Jerusalem nor Rome but a
universal symbol of a fleshly minded world, and its
seven kings symbolize the entire succession of earthly

power. With great insight, John points to an eighth king—the beast, or Satan, who belongs to the seven (Rev. 17:11). As the eighth king appearing beyond history, he'll be the ultimate monarch sentenced at the last judgment. His influence over the world's order is why he also belongs to the seven.

John also sees ten "rulers" with no kingdoms. *Ten* symbolizes finality, and these pathetic weaklings epitomize the final collapse of earthly presumption. Though at war with the Lamb, they immediately fail at His appearing—not because He overcomes them in battle but because He is King of Kings and Lord of Lords! (Rev. 17:12-14). Jesus will not have to earn His authority at history's close. He has it now, and His presence will vanquish Babylon and all servants of the beast instantaneously.

Earth's Lament and Heaven's Joy

"When the kings of the earth who committed adultery with her and shared her luxury see the smoke of her burning, they will weep and mourn over her. Terrified at her torment, they will stand far off and cry; 'Woe! Woe, O great city, O Babylon, city of power! In one hour your doom has come!'" (Rev. 18:9,10).

Hallelujah! The smoke from her goes up for ever and ever...Let us rejoice and be glad and give him glory! For the wedding of the Lamb has come, and his bride has made herself ready (Rev. 19:3,7).

This vision contrasts judgment and redemption through bitter tears and shouts of joy. Kings, merchants and shipmasters wail over Babylon's fall (Rev. 18:9-19), but they weep only for themselves. The rewards of commerce in Babylon are gone, and they're left destitute. Insightfully, John lists merchants' inventories, including things normally associated with first century affluence—gold, silver, precious stones, pearls, fine linens, spices and other items of luxury. The list also includes the "*bodies and souls of men*" (Rev. 18:13). Is he saying those who live exclusively for so-called "good things" pay for them with their souls?

As John watches, innumerable hosts in heaven exult in the harlot's fall (Rev. 19:1-3). If she symbolized a secular, political empire, their vindictiveness might be embarrassing, but Babylon is the kingdom of the flesh and represents a frontal attack on divinity. God is omnipotent! Sin says, "I will displace Him and be my own god." God is omnipresent! Sin says, "I will live as if He did not exist." God is omniscient! Sin says, "I know better than He does!" Sin curses the whole order of creation, and man's subservience to the harlot of fleshly desires is that order's most odious prospect. The smoke of Babylon rising forever is a symbol of eternal redress that causes angels to rejoice. Having considered the work of God's hands and the excellence of His name in all the earth, they've waited to see His purpose in creation restored and urge us to rejoice over Babylon's fall (Rev. 18:5). Why not? The demise of self-exaltation and sinful presumption *is* cause for joy.

In contrast to Babylon's judgment, John sees redemption in the beautiful image of a bride of the Lamb, and the prospect of her wedding is cause for even greater joy (Rev. 18:6-9). Unlike the harlot, who is garish, overstated, decadent and gaudily ornate, her only attribute is the fine linen of purity, and her suitability as the bride of Christ is determined by the characteristic most complementary to Him—holiness! This imagery points to God's loving purpose in creation.

Contrary to a fundamental assumption of western culture, creation is an issue for theology rather than science, because it expresses God's character. He is love, and, by definition, love seeks an object. Before time began, divine love infused energy into the universe's formless void with the words *"Let there be light"* (Gen. 1:3). Words presuppose an audience and prove a divine heart was reaching out. The universe would be a house in which He could dwell in love with a creature bearing His image and capable of replying.

The universe was an expression of His infinite perfection and glory, and its excellence charmed angels, but starry heavens couldn't return a complementary voice to God, and love's handiwork wasn't concluded. He spoke again, saying, *"Let us make man in our image"* (Gen. 1:26). He would create man to express His love.

Life is not the product of an accident in space but a gift of love. Its initial manifestation was fellowship in Eden. Its ultimate manifestation is a Redeemer who restores our fellowship with God. Those who respond to His love and experience it await His return as eagerly as a pure and holy bride waits for her bridegroom's appearing.

The Vision in Perspective

Then a mighty angel picked up a boulder the size of a large millstone and threw it into the sea, and said: "With such violence the great city of Babylon will be thrown down, never to be found again" (Rev. 18:21).

Who is Babylon? Who is the harlot called "Mystery" enticing the world as the mother of all abominations? Who intoxicates kings and merchants as the goddess of pride and vanity? Who is Babylon but the flesh exulting in itself? Who is she but the mindset that replaces love for God with carnal pride? Who is she but the personification of a world obsessed with self-indulgence?

John's stentorian tones and compelling imagery are so powerful that they lead some to conjure violent earthly conflagrations between future tyrants, apostate popes or diabolical empires to explain them, but his graphic images of a bride and a prostitute are symbols of spiritual, rather than political, realities. The bride waiting for her wedding day is a picture of the kingdom of grace. The prostitute with no prospect but destruction is a picture of the world's fleshliness. She will be exposed as a cheap harlot rejected by her clients, and those deceived by her will despise the wine that intoxicated them and turn their wrath inward. John sees them turn on her to eat her flesh and burn her with fire (Rev. 17:16).

These images carve a clear distinction between the calling of God and the enticements of the flesh. Seen in isolation, Babylon can be deceitfully seductive. Seen in truth, it is doomed and headed for destruction. The city where smoking ruins sit in eerie silence and lamps are forever dimmed isn't some sinister future world order or a dust-covered reflection of ancient Rome. Babylon isn't a world we don't know but the one we do know, and the symbols describing it are timeless. Its music will be heard no more! Its workmen will ply their trade no more! Its millstones will no longer grind out wheat for daily bread. Its lamps will never be lit, and brides and grooms will never be seen within it again (Rev. 18:22-23).

Today, music plays in the midst of Babylon as her brides and grooms plan their futures. Millstones grind continually as workmen look for more lucrative profits. The lamps of wealth, pleasure and self-interest shine brightly in her streets, but a world devoted to indulgence without integrity and to passion without love is a harlot inviting us to take pleasure in spite of the consequences. Like a deceitful temptress offering easy gratification, she plies her trade in every corner of the globe, constantly extending a wanton hand with a golden chalice and inviting us to drink more deeply. She masters the art of seduction and easily sways those who fix their gaze on her, but her offer is a betrayal and her wine is poisoned. John warns,

"Don't be intoxicated by Babylon! Her doom is sealed. Come out from her! Do not share in her sins! We are called to be the bride of the Lamb!"

Chapter 12

John's Seventh Vision— Victorious Living
Part 1: An Enemy Bound

And I saw an angel coming down out of heaven, having the key to the Abyss and holding in his hand a great chain. He seized the dragon, that ancient serpent, who is the devil, or Satan, and bound him for a thousand years. He threw him into the Abyss, and locked and sealed it over him (Rev. 20:1-3).

Recommended Reading:
Chapters 19 and 20 of Revelation

In an earlier vision of the world's condition, Satan, a fallen angel, was given the key to the abyss and released a torrent of deception (Rev. 9:11). In glorious testimony to the truth that sets men free, Johns now sees Jesus as a conquering warrior, binding Satan in an abyss for a figurative "*thousand years*," representing the lifespan of the Church on earth. Perhaps John's imagery was inspired in part by a passage from Jude's epistle: "*And the angels who did not keep their positions of authority but abandoned their own home— these he has kept in darkness, bound with everlasting chains for judgment on the great Day*" (Jude 6).

In any case, this scene consummates a scriptural

theme. After the fall in Eden, God promised to bruise the serpent's head with the seed of a woman (Gen. 3:15, NKJV). To the patriarchs, that seed was the "*Root of David,*" ruling with a rod of iron. The prophet foresaw a warrior "*Traveling in the greatness of His strength...speak[ing] in righteousness, mighty to save*" (Isa. 63:1, NKJV). The psalmist foresaw the ascended King of Glory, "*The LORD strong and mighty, the LORD mighty in battle*" (Ps. 24:8). In the New Testament, John the Apostle confirmed our Lord's mission: "*The reason the Son of God appeared was to destroy the devil's work*" (1 John 3:8).

Jesus defined His crucifixion as a judgement and defeat for Satan: "*Now is the time for judgment on this world; now the prince of this world will be driven out*" (John 12:31). At His ascension, He confirmed His victory: "*All authority in heaven and on earth has been given to me*" (Matt. 28:18). He gave his disciples a mandate for hope with the words "*I have overcome the world*" (John 16:33).

Jewish messianic thought often portrayed the Messiah as both warrior and bridegroom. The Church is the bride of Christ, and John sees her warrior bridegroom called "*Faithful and True*" on a white horse as a conqueror in a triumphal procession (Rev. 19:11). Echoing Isaiah, John says the warrior has trodden the winepress of the fury of God's wrath (Rev. 19:15) and His robe is dipped in blood (Rev. 19:13). Jesus experienced that fury and dipped His robes in blood at Calvary but emerged victorious.

He is God incarnate, and no single title can fully reveal the scope of His divine majesty. Because He is the fulfillment of all promise, John ascribes to Him numerous titles taken from Scripture. In another reference to the "Root of David," John says He rules with an "*iron scepter*" (Rev. 19:15). He is also the "*Word of God*" (Rev. 19:13)—the tangible expression of an unseen God—and "*KING OF KINGS AND LORD OF LORDS*" (Rev. 19:16). These titles acquaint us with aspects of our Lord's divinity, but, as mortals, we can never fully comprehend it. In the end, John tells us that our conquering warrior alone knows His name (Rev. 19:12). God once described Himself by saying; "I AM THAT I AM!" (Exod. 3:14, KJV). No finite model can ever describe an infinite God.

Resurrected, Reigning and Serving

"I saw thrones on which were seated those who had been given authority to judge...They came to life and reigned with Christ a thousand years" (Rev. 20:4).

In view of Jesus' victory over sin, death and hell, John sees believers as resurrected, reigning and serving. Paul also spoke of resurrection to Christians in Ephesus and Rome: "*As for you, you were dead in your transgressions and sins...But because of his great love for us, God, who is rich in mercy, made us alive with Christ even when we were dead in transgressions*" (Eph. 2:1,4,5). "*We were therefore buried with him through baptism into death in order that, just as Christ was raised from the dead through the glory of the Father, we too may live a new life*" (Rom. 6:4,5).

Believers lead men to God and declare God to men, and John sees them as priests. Priesthood is about service—not status. Even in exile, John dedicated Revelation to the One who "*has made us to be a kingdom and priests*" (Rev. 1:6) and wrote later: "*with your blood you purchased men for God from every tribe and language and people and nation. You have made them to be a kingdom and priests to serve our God*" (Rev. 5:9,10).

Satan's binding (Rev. 20:1-2) testifies to Jesus' victory at Calvary. The imagery isn't literal, since Satan isn't a dragon but a spirit that can't be confined physically. Using consistent rules of interpretation, "*a thousand years*," or 10 x 10 x 10, aren't literal either. They symbolize the Church's life on earth during which our Lord's power holds Satan in check.

Those who see this 1,000 years as a literal future millennium usually compartmentalize history into seven ages or "dispensations," claiming separate plans of salvation based on law, grace or works apply to each. That unscriptural view removes Jesus as the only sufficient sacrifice for sin. Scripture knows only one Savior and faithfully proclaims Him in every age. All that went before anticipates Him and all that came after testifies to Him. Paul's case for justification by faith in Romans rests entirely on the example of Abraham's faith thousands of years before (Rom. 4). He saw no disconnection between Abraham's justifying faith and ours.

Dispensationalists confine salvation by faith in Jesus to a "Church age," which they see as a parenthesis in a historical view dominated by Israel. They

claim that age—and the Spirit's ministry in conversion—will end when a "secret rapture" carries the
Church to heaven. History will then converge on
Israel during a three-and-one-half-year or seven-
year "Tribulation period." Allegedly, Revelation's
scenes of judgment are coded pictures of Jesus
slaughtering Israel's enemies prior to returning the
Church to earth to oversee an earthly kingdom head-
quartered in Jerusalem for 1,000 years.

To explain John's scenes of redemption, dispensationalists invent "Tribulation saints," claiming
some who resist the Spirit during the "Church age"
and miss "the Rapture" will save themselves during
this "Tribulation" by reading Scripture or refusing
satanic tattoos. Reading Scripture in any age won't
change its message! It offers no plan of self-wrought
salvation, says the arm of flesh will never save (2
Chron. 32:8) and that no one comes to the Father
unless the Spirit draws him (John 6:44). It makes
rejecting the Holy Spirit unpardonable in this age or
in the age to come. Since no one can ever save themselves, John's scenes of redemption can't be future
ages peopled by self-saved "Tribulation saints."

The cardinal rule of hermeneutics says valid
interpretations must agree with Scripture, but dispensational thinking consistently disagrees. Jesus'
death broke down walls of partition between Jew and
Gentile (Eph. 2:14-18), but dispensationalists confer
preferred status on Israel and replace the kingdom
Jesus said wasn't of this world (John 18:36) with a
future earthly regime—for which there's no need,
time or place in the plan of salvation. Dispensational

theory appears to make satanic deception a form of external propaganda to be somehow isolated from sinful human nature in a future millennium. Satanic deception isn't external! It's rooted in the reprobate mind described by James: "*But each one is tempted when, by his own evil desire, he is dragged away and enticed. Then, after desire has conceived, it gives birth to sin; and sin, when it is full-grown, gives birth to death*" (Jas. 1:14,15).

If people in a future millennium sinned in thought, word or deed, satanic deception would still control them. If they didn't, they'd no longer be sinners by nature. Dispensational theory can't explain either scenario but denigrates Jesus' perfect atonement for sin, insisting animal sacrifices will again be offered in a restored temple, even though Scripture clearly declares such sacrifices forever powerless and obsolete:

> *The law is only a shadow of the good things that are coming—not the realties themselves. For this reason it can never, by the same sacrifices repeated endlessly year after year, make perfect those who draw near to worship* (Heb. 10:1).

God never contradicts His Word, and His only remedy for sin is the cross of Jesus Christ.

In perspective, the dispensational view of believers returned from heaven in immortal bodies, "Tribulation saints" in mortal bodies and sinless sinners freed of satanic deception spending 1,000 years offering worthless sacrifices in a restored Jewish temple for sins they no longer commit should be self-evidently absurd! More sensibly, this millennium symbolizes the life of the Church freed from Satan's lies, resurrected with Jesus and serving Him as a royal priesthood.

At the Day of Atonement's final service, all prayers began with "Seal us O Lord in your book of life," John refers to the "*seal of God*" (Rev. 9:4). That is the indwelling presence of His Holy Spirit. John also speaks of a "*second death*" (Rev. 20:6,14,18). A life of sin is spiritual death, leading inevitably to the "second death" of a lost eternity from which there's no redemption. John sees history's all powerful Judge on a great white throne with the dead, great and small, before Him. As the books are opened, the unsaved reap sin's final wage and join Satan in a "*lake of fire*" (Rev. 20:11-15).

Loosing Satan and the Forces of Evil

When the thousand years are over, Satan will be released from his prison and will go out to deceive the nations (Rev. 20:7,8).

The Church's figurative thousand-year life ends when our Lord returns. On a great and final day, Satan will be loosed, but his release will be a short ride to damnation. God is perfect in holiness, and His purposes will never harmonize with Satan's. As Jesus told Pharisees, a house divided can't stand! (Matt. 12:25). Satan's "release" will send him to a final judgment along with all of his servants. It recalls Passover when Pharaoh's horsemen were dispatched on a last mission and galloped to their deaths.

John calls Satan's servants *"Gog and Magog"* (Rev. 20:8). This ancient term draws on Judaism's messianic beliefs, which, though very diverse, share some elements. Rabbi Louis Jacobs explains:

> Biblical (messianic) ideas were embellished in the Apocrypha and Pseudopigrapha so that there was forged a complete chain of messianic specu- lation...they reappear in order in the rabbinic lit- erature. The links are: the signs of the Messiah; the birth pangs of the Messiah; the coming of Elijah; the trumpet of the Messiah; the ingath- ering of the exiles; the reception of proselytes; the war with Gog and Magog; the days of the Messiah; the renovation of the world; the day of judgment; the resurrection of the dead; the world to come.[24]

Most links in this chain appear in Revelation in some form, including terminology about Gog and Magog. The tenth chapter of Genesis listed "Magog" as one of Japeth's sons along with "Meshech" and "Tubal." Their names were linked later to the Assyrian centers of "Muschu" and "Tabal," and the term "Gog and Magog" became a synonym for Israel's northern enemies. Ezekiel denounced "Gog" (Ezek. 38)—probably a region occupied by Magog's descen- dants—but the identity of a specific nation with known boundaries is lost in antiquity. John sees "Gog and Magog" as a universal synonym for evil in "*the four corners of the earth,*" (Rev. 20:8) perishing with Satan in the fires of hell.

The Vision in Perspective

> *Blessed and holy are those who have part in the first resurrection. The second death has no power over them* (Rev. 20:6).

Faith is the victory that overcomes the world, because Jesus' death and resurrection bruised the serpent's head (Gen. 3:15, NKJV), led captivity captive (Eph. 4:8, NKJV) and made His enemies His footstool (Heb. 10:13), reserved in chains unto everlasting judgment. Despite tyrannical persecution or the seductiveness of evil, Jesus' cross and resurrection make victorious living possible and final victory certain! He has subdued the foe!

This hope energized early Christians, and it still resonates. Jesus is the eternal Word of God to a fallen world, and He reigns with an iron scepter (Rev. 19:15), judges justly (Rev. 19:11) and wears many crowns (Rev. 19:12). When He ascended to the right hand of the Father, heaven's everlasting doors were lifted to welcome a Conqueror called "*Faithful and True*" (Rev. 19:11). The Lord strong and mighty, the Lord mighty in battle and the King of Glory (Ps. 24:8) entered. The One before whom heaven's gates were lifted is also the One against whom hell's gates can never prevail! (Matt. 16:18, NKJV). Heaven's angels bow before Him, and hell's angels fear Him and flee!

His victory is vicarious, and we live according to the limitless power of His resurrection. Our names aren't in earthly registries according to race and nationality but in an eternal "*book of life*" (Rev. 20:12,15). We aren't pawns in earthly struggles with outcomes yet pending but kings and priests (Rev. 5:10, NKJV) serving God and humanity. Freed from deception, we've passed from death unto life (1 John 3:14), and our faith rests on a truth earth's trials and Satan's cunning can't erase. The tomb is empty! Satan is bound, and Jesus is Lord!

Chapter 13

John's Seventh Vision— Victorious Living
Part 2: A Holy City

I saw the Holy City, the new Jerusalem, coming down out of heaven from God, prepared as a bride beautifully dressed for her husband (Rev. 21:2).

Recommended Reading:
Chapters 21 and 22 of Revelation

This vision draws on Judaism's deeply rooted concept of a "Jerusalem above." Jews believe the temple replicated the heavenly court and also see Jerusalem as the earthly manifestation of a heavenly reality. "Next year in Jerusalem" is a popular phrase among them, and they build synagogues so anyone entering the door is facing that city.[25]

Early Christians knew Jesus' death and resurrection changed the rules. God's kingdom wasn't about an earthly city but about spiritual rebirth, and the Church saw itself as a "holy city born from above" even before the earthly Jerusalem's destruction. For example, the author of Hebrews spoke of redemption as a heavenly Jerusalem: "*But you have come to Mount Zion, to the heavenly Jerusalem, the city of the living God"* (Heb. 12:22).

In language Jews would regard as heresy, Paul equated Israel with Arabia and Jerusalem with slavery but called the Church the *"Jerusalem that is above"*: *"Now Hagar stands for Mount Sinai in Arabia and corresponds to the present city of Jerusalem, because she is in slavery with her children. But the Jerusalem that is above is free, and she is our mother"* (Gal. 4:25-26). His epistle to Ephesus praised God who *"has blessed us in the heavenly realms with every spiritual blessing in Christ"* (Eph. 1:3). In words oft confused for a reference to heaven, he told Corinth the Holy Spirit's presence is a fore-taste of paradise:

> *No eye has seen, no ear has heard, no mind has conceived what God has prepared for those who love him,"—but God has revealed it to us by his Spirit...We have not received the spirit of the world but the Spirit who is from God, that we may understand what God has freely given us* (1 Cor. 2:9,10,12).

After seeing the conquering bridegroom, John sees the Church as *"a bride beautifully dressed for her husband"* and as a holy Jerusalem coming down to earth from above (Rev. 21:2). In an implicit con-trast with Babylon, an angel repeats the phrase that signaled Babylon's judgment, *"Come, I will show you"* (Rev. 21:9;17:1), but this time John sees a holy place of paradisiacal serenity where tears, death, sorrow and crying are no more and from which the "*cowardly, unbelieving, abominable, murderers, sexually immoral, sorcerers, idolaters, and all liars*" (Rev. 21:8, NKJV) are excluded. Just as Babylon, born from below, is the fleshliness of the world, the city born from above is the essence of holiness.

Isaiah prophesied Jerusalem's rebuilding after its destruction, telling the people to "*Arise, shine, for your light has come*" (Isa. 60:1). The nations would walk by that light, and their children would be gathered from afar to live in the "*City of the LORD*" (Isa. 60:14). Its walls and gates, called "*Salvation*" and "*Praise*" (Isa. 60:18), would never close, and its citizens would be called "*The Holy People, The Redeemed of the LORD...Sought Out, A City Not Forsaken*" (Isa. 62:12, NKJV). In John's day, Jerusalem was a pile of rubble and its gates were abandoned, but he knew the city born from above and "*Redeemed of the LORD*" was the blood-washed Church.

Gates and Foundations

On the gates were written the names of the twelve tribes of Israel. There were three gates on the east, three on the north, three on the south and three on the west. The wall of the city had twelve foundations, and on them were the names of the twelve apostles of the Lamb...The foundations of the city's walls were decorated with every kind of precious stone. The first foundation was jasper, the second sapphire, the third chalcedony, the fourth emerald, the

> *fifth sardonyx, the sixth carnelian, the seventh chrysolite, the eighth beryl, the ninth topaz, the tenth chrysoprase, the eleventh jacinth, and the twelfth amethyst. The twelve gates were twelve pearls: each individual gate was of one pearl. And the street of the city was pure gold, like transparent glass* (Rev. 21:13,14,19-21).

During Babylonian captivity, Ezekiel prophesied a restored Jerusalem with gates bearing Israel's tribal names (Ezek. 48:31). John sees the real meaning of the prophecy. Israel was the channel through which Jesus came, and His city's gates would bear its tribal names, but His gates tell a larger story. They're made of pearl—a substance oysters produce through a process involving suffering and blood. These gates are formed by the suffering and blood of the Redeemer and face all directions, offering access to earth's four corners.

John sees a foundation of precious stones. He draws on three sources—priestly vestments, Isaiah's prophecy and a reference from St. Paul. High priests wore a breastplate of twelve stones signifying Israel's twelve tribes.[26] Rabbis felt the stones had two functions. When the priest entered the Holy of Holies, they would remind him of his role as intercessor and would also call God's attention to the plight of Israel. The stones John sees are similar to those worn by priests, but the imagery is hyperbole, exalting the holy city's magnificence. Isaiah described Jerusalem as having a foundation of precious stones (Isa. 54:11), and Paul said the Church was "*built on the foundation of the apostles and prophets, with Christ Jesus himself as the chief cornerstone*" (Eph. 2:20). Our faith rests on that precious foundation!

A Three Dimensional City of Light

The city was laid out like a square, as long as it was wide. He measured the city with the rod and found it to be 12,000 stadia in length, and as wide and high as it is long...The city does not need the sun or the moon to shine on it, for the glory of God gives it light, and the Lamb is its lamp (Rev. 21:16,23).

The holy city's length, breadth and height are equal. Babylon, the kingdom of the flesh, measures solely by momentary pleasure or material gain. Babylonians hold time too closely to the eye to see eternity and know only the two dimensions of time and space. Citizens of the holy city "*together with all the saints...grasp how wide and long and high and deep is the love of Christ, and to know this love that surpasses knowledge*" (Eph. 3:18-19). Their goals, priorities, choices and affections are opened upward, adding a third dimension to their living.

The Lamb is the light of the holy city. At Sinai, Moses' face shone with divine glory after only a partial revelation of it (Exod. 34:29-30). Jesus perfectly manifests the glory of the only begotten Son, "*full of grace and truth*" (John 1:14). As the true light lighting all men, He, alone can say; "*I am the light of the world*" (John 8:12;9:5). His followers don't walk in darkness, because He is the light in their midst (John 8:12). As "*children of light*" (Eph. 5:8), they stand with Him on a holy Mt. Zion where His radiance is more brilliant than the sun, moon and stars.

A River and Trees

> *Then the angel showed me the river of the water of life, as clear as crystal, flowing from the throne of God and of the Lamb down the middle of the great street of the city. On each side of the river stood the tree of life, bearing twelve crops of fruit, yielding its fruit every month. And the leaves of the tree are for the healing of the nations* (Rev. 22:1,2).

Inside the holy city's walls, John sees no dazzling architecture. No spectacular public galleries, libraries, capitols, courthouses or skyscrapers fill its skyline. Freeways, harbors and airports are invisible. Stadiums and arenas can't be found. Historic and cultural monuments normally visible in great cities are absent. Curiously, the prominent features of a city born from above with jeweled foundations, fabulous gates and golden pavement are a crystal river flowing from God's throne and trees.

Water can create lush gardens amid barren sands, and Scripture constantly uses it as a symbol of grace. The psalmist said, "*with you is the fountain of life*" (Ps. 36:9) and spoke of "*a river whose streams make glad the city of God*") (Ps. 46:4). Joel said a fountain would "*flow out of the LORD's house*" (Joel

3:18) and Zechariah prophesied "*living water will flow out from Jerusalem*" (Zech. 14:8). Jesus said "*rivers of living water*" (John 7:38, NKJV) would flow from His followers' inner beings. Babylon's wine has no life-giving quality, but the crystal river of grace flowing from God's throne nourishes beautiful trees in the holy city.

The fall separated man from God, and he lost access to the tree of life. In the holy city, John sees his access restored. Beside grace's infinite river, the tree produces leaves to heal nations. This isn't a picture of heaven. When time is no more, earth's nations will no longer exist to require healing, but, in this world, the godly are like trees planted by a river of grace, bringing forth fruit in due season (Ps. 1:3). The river sustains them, and their leaves heal because holiness and wholeness are inextricably linked. Wherever one finds holiness, one finds the healing of the human soul.

The Vision in Perspective

He said to me: "It is done. I am the Alpha and the Omega, the Beginning and the End. To him who is thirsty I will give to drink without cost from the spring of the water of life" (Rev 21:6).

The Christian's ultimate prize is eternal union with the Lord in a paradise where sorrow, sighing, sickness and suffering are no more (Rev. 21:4). Death and defilement will only be memories, but the riches of grace aren't reserved exclusively for heaven.

In this vision, John sees its future glory, but he also sees the present glory of redemption as he catches a glimpse of a holy city rising on the banks of the river of grace. Heaven will be holy living above. Holy living in the power of the Spirit is a foretaste of heaven below, and John sees the magnificence of both!

God's people, living in heavenly places in Christ, are now the earthly manifestation of the "*Jerusalem above*" (Gal. 4:26, NKJV). Jesus' sacrifice is their gate of entry, His power is their cornerstone, and His glory is the light in their midst. Redeemed, sought out and not forsaken, they dwell within walls of divine providence resting on precious foundations set by prophets and apostles. Inside gates called "*Salvation*" and "*Praise*," they walk streets paved with gold tried in the fire as God refines them by His Spirit. Sustained by the river of grace, they drink without cost from the spring of the water of life. Abiding in the vine, they bear fruit that heals nations. Eternity will consummate the fellowship begun here, but, in heaven or on earth, a holy city of the redeemed appears as a bride adorned for her husband whenever Jesus rules and reigns!

Chapter 14

What Does It All Mean?

The angel said to me, "These words are trustworthy and true...Behold, I am coming soon!...And behold, I am coming quickly, and My reward is with Me" (Rev. 22:6,7,12, NKJV).

Recommended Reading:
Chapters 22 of Revelation

The powerful images John records aren't coded messages meant to inspire fantasies about future wars or final conflagrations. They can't be understood by slotting them into imaginary events in our unknowable tomorrows or conjuring future battles between earthly armies. Media reports and press clippings don't explain them. Fictitious timetables, date setting and sensational speculation completely miss their point. They can't be deciphered by self-proclaimed "experts in Bible prophecy" who regularly predict raptures that never come, label dozens of world leaders as antichrists and forecast end times battles based on power blocs that vanish from history's stage every few decades. Without exception, history has shown such decoding exercises failed to grasp the trends of the present, the events of the future or the meaning of Scripture that clearly teaches that the hour of our Lord's return is both unknown and unknowable.

God's Word isn't a code book but an open book. It wasn't written to mystify but to guide, and it's trustworthy and true. The power of John's imagery lies not in mystery but in familiarity. Apocalyptic horsemen, representing the corruption of human power, appear on nightly newscasts to mark the world's self-inflicted wounds. Legions of death angels claim a daily harvest of souls and remind us that life is finite. Earthly disasters that should bring men to repentance often invoke only their blasphemies. A culture that mocks purity, exalts the ego and urges us to live wantonly is a seductive harlot peddling fleshly wares on every street corner. Like a diabolical beast, it spews contempt on all things godly.

John's visions also confront us with counsel and hope. Seven churches mirror common challenges to faith and consecration. Angels opening seals show the plight of the ungodly. Trumpets and plagues issue calls to repentance. The measurement of the inner court invites self-examination. A woman sustained in the wilderness shows God's faithfulness. The deceitful beasts of secular values and false religion prove the need for faith, endurance and singleness of purpose. Babylon's destruction exposes the vanity of worldly pursuits. The harvest of the earth points to a final judgment. A redeemed host stands before God in triumph. If these things show our world as it is, how will it end? What does our Lord mean when He warns us that He will come quickly (Rev. 22:20, NKJV)?

One Final Day

Scripture repeatedly points to a great and final "day of the Lord" when the last trumpet will sound and the ruler of time and space will roll the heavens back as a scroll. With incomprehensible condescension, the "*Root and the Offspring of David*" (Rev. 22:16) once came meekly to earth as a sacrificial Lamb, and His crucifixion opened the veil to the Holy of Holies. On earth's final day, He'll open the veil of eternity and judge the wicked with the breath of His lips. At the dawn of creation, those lips spoke the universe into existence. A minute particle of dust, invisible to the human eye, forms a larger part of the earth than earth does of the heavens created then. Our Lord isn't a puny being who must win future earthly battles to prove His authority. When He appears, the sheer force of His majesty will cause every knee to bow. On a single day, He will destroy principalities and powers, including death itself, and place all things under his feet. Paul said that day will come without warning: "*The day of the Lord will come like a thief in the night*" (1 Thess. 5:2).

Peter gave more detail: "*But the day of the Lord will come like a thief. The heavens will disappear with a roar; the elements will be destroyed by fire, and the earth and everything in it will be laid bare*" (2 Pet. 3:10).

On the day that concludes the business of time and

eternity, every soul that has ever lived will give an accounting, including the resurrected dead. Paul affirms the point: *"For the Lord himself will come down from heaven, with a loud command, with the voice of the archangel and with the trumpet call of God, and the dead in Christ will rise first"* (1 Thess. 4:16). In John's Gospel, Jesus spoke of resurrection four times, saying, *"I shall…raise them up at the last day"* (John 6:39) and *"I will raise him up at the last day"* (John 6:40,44,54).

Righteousness cries out for an ultimate vindication, and evil demands an ultimate condemnation. Jesus said earth's last day will bring judgment: *"There is a judge for the one who rejects me and does not accept my words; that very word which I spoke will condemn him at the last day"* (John 12:48).

On another occasion, He was more descriptive:

> *"Many will say to me on that day, 'Lord, Lord, did we not prophesy in your name, and in your name drive out demons and perform many miracles?' Then I will tell them plainly, 'I never knew you. Away from me, you evildoers!'"* (Matt. 7:22,23).

When our Lord judges evil, He'll also vindicate righteousness. Paul tells the Corinthians: *"He will keep you strong to the end, so that you will be blameless on the day of our Lord Jesus Christ"* (1 Cor. 1:8).

Looking forward in hope, Paul says to Timothy: *"Now there is in store for me the crown of righteousness, which the Lord, the righteous Judge, will award to me on that day—and not only to me, but also to all who have longed for his appearing"* (2 Tim. 4:8).

Scripture's witness is consistent and clear! Nothing need be added to it, and nothing should ever be taken from it (Rev. 22:18-19). On a single day, our Lord will appear, time will cease, the planets will vanish, the living and dead will be judged and the righteous rewarded. All the business of time will be resolved, culminating in a glorious coronation as Jesus is crowned King of Kings and Lord of Lords:

> *The seventh angel sounded his trumpet, and there were loud voices in heaven, which said: "The kingdom of the world has become the kingdom of our Lord and of his Christ, and he will reign for ever and ever"* (Rev. 11:15).

A Final Perspective

> *"Let him who does wrong continue to do wrong; let him who is vile continue to be vile; let him who does right continue to do right; and let him who is holy continue to be holy"* (Rev. 22:11).

We need no special prophetic insights to discern history's close, and John doesn't call us to arrange combatants like toy soldiers on an imaginary "end times" battlefield. Instead, he calls us to prepare for our Lord's appearing and to be vigilant in the battle for souls already underway. Ever since man's fall in Eden, an eternal liar has deceived billions into following him blindly into hell. John points to a Redeemer and pleads with us to serve Him with persevering faith and trust.

Future events won't determine history's outcome!
Jesus' cross and resurrection already have, and they
will be our ultimate measure! Some day, He will
appear as unexpectedly as a thief comes in the night
(1 Thess. 5:2; 2 Pet. 3:10). On that day, people will
be eating and drinking, marrying and giving in mar-
riage (Matt. 24:37-39) and doing what's right in their
own eyes. Many will live as if God does not exist,
indulging trivial, self-serving preoccupations mea-
surable only by their insignificance against the back-
drop of eternity. Suddenly and without warning, the
sound of a last trumpet will call them to account.

Instinctively, we know something in our universe
is less than perfect. We shun talk of judgment—
except for the sins of others—but we readily embrace
redemption. Our dilemma arises from knowing
where to find it. As the twentieth century dawned,
we thought we were our own redeemers. Modernism
was intellectually chic, and it told us progress and
technology coupled with political and economic
reform were humanity's saviors—until unprece-
dented inhumanity shattered its presumption.

After gazing at the blood filling trenches in two
world wars, sifting the charred bones at Auschwitz
and contemplating nuclear devastation, we replaced
modernism's failed gospel with the vacuous moods of
postmodernism. Now we declare God and truth
unknowable and pretentiously claim to embrace all
things equally. Our theme song is "Celebrate diversity!" but the tune is already playing in a minor key.
The World Trade Center's smoldering ashes, a nuclear
threat in North Korea, genocide in Africa and suicide

bombers in the Middle East prove many things under the world's diverse umbrella aren't cause for celebration. We'll drop postmodernism's incoherence more quickly in this century than we discarded modernism's presumption in the last, but we'll never perfect our world!

Many centuries ago, a forgotten exile saw the truth we miss. Redemption isn't found in the scrolls of philosophers but in a Redeemer who can open the scroll revealing God's mind and heart! He speaks with supreme authority as the eternal One *"who was, and is, and is to come"* (Rev. 4:8). When our presumption has been exhausted, His Word will stand firm. It's never abstract or subject to intellectual fads. He simply calls us to Himself.

Superior to angels, patriarchs and all things in creation, He commands the elements at His will. The keeper of eternity's keys is a triumphant Lamb on Mt. Zion whose blood washes life's soiled garments white. He is a compassionate High Priest who knows our works and raises the fallen! He's the conquering Warrior who'll forever vanquish Satan's works by the simple fact of His presence, and He's the Alpha and Omega who'll say a final *"It is done!"* to bring history to a close. He's a Bridegroom preparing a holy place for a holy bride, and someday, He'll gather a redeemed multitude from earth's four corners to be the Scepter ruling over them in righteousness.

Until then, His people are faithful witnesses living holy lives on holy ground. His standard flies over them in a verdant wilderness where insidious floods do not threaten and hideous beasts cannot destroy. In an inner court of true worship, they offer themselves as first fruits and living sacrifices. As trees planted by the river of grace, they produce fruit unto holiness, and someday they'll wave palms of victory in a never-ending triumph.

Until the day judgment and redemption are concluded, we must choose between the vile and the holy. Babylon seductively offers a golden cup of fleshly enticements, but its price is steep and its contents poisoned. In the holy city of redemption, a pure and endless river of life flows from the throne of a Redeemer. His offer can be trusted!

> *"Come!" Whoever is thirsty, let him come; and whoever wishes, let him take the free gift of the water of life* (Rev. 22:17).

Endnotes

[1] T.S. Eliot, *The Sacred Wood:Essays on Poetry and Criticism* (Methune, London, 1920

[2] Alfred Edersheim, *The Temple, Its Ministry and Services* (Montville: Hendrickson Publishers, 1994) p. 37.

[3] Irwin P. Goodenough, *Jewish Symbols in the Graeco Roman Period*, Princeton University Press, Princeton, 1953 p. 28

[4] Isaiah 1:18, Leviticus 16:20-26

[5] *Hastings Dictionary of the Bible*, Hendrickson Publishers Inc., 2003

[6] *Against Heresies*, Volume 1, p. 351-352

[7] Rabbi Joseph Telushkin, *Biblical Literacy*, William Morrow and company, New York, 1997 p. 551

[8] Rabbi Abraham Witty, *Exploring Jewish Tradition*, Doubleday, New York, 2001 p. 52

[9] Ismar Elbogen, *Jewish Liturgy, A Comprehensive History*, trans. Raymond Scheindlin (Philadelphia: The Jewish Publication Society, 1993) p. 190.

[10] Rabbi Joseph Telushkin, *Jewish Literacy*, William Morrow and company, New York, 1991 p. 651

[11] Jonathan Sacks, *A Letter in the Scroll* (New York:

The Free Press, 2000) p. 39.

[12] Kevin Harris, *The Wit and Wisdom of Albert Einstein*, web site 1995

[13] Irving M. Zeitlin, *Ancient Judaism*, Polity Press, Oxford, 1984 p. 23

[14] Rabbi Joseph Telushkin, *Jewish Literacy*, William Morrow and Company, New York, 1991 p. 564-570

[15] Rabbi Joseph Telushkin, *Jewish Literacy*, William Morrow and Company, New York, 1991 p. 564-570

[16] Isaac Klein, *Guide to Jewish Religious Practice* (New York: The Jewish Theological Seminary of America, 1979

[17] Yehezkel Kaufmann, *The Religion of Israel* (Chicago: The University of Chicago Press, 1960) p. 303.

[18] Kaufman, p. 64.

[19] Isaac Klein, *Guide to Jewish Religious Practice* (New York: The Jewish Theological Seminary of America, 1979 p. 191.

[20] Joseph Heineman, *Literature of the Synagogue*, (New York, Behrman House Inc., 1975) p. 303,

[21] William Barclay, *The Revelation of John Volume 1*, Westminster Press, Philadelphia, 1976

[22] Rabbi Abraham Witty, *Exploring Jewish Tradition*, Doubleday, New York, 2001 p. 27

[23] Rabbi Joseph Telushkin, *Jewish Literacy*, William Morrow and Company, New York, 1991 p. 270

[24] Louis Jacobs, *A Jewish Theology*, (London: Darton, Longman and Todd, 1973) p. 293,294.

[25] Raphael Posner, Uri Kaploun, Shalom Cohen, *Jewish Liturgy*, Ketter Publishing House, Jerusalem, 1975 p. 32

[26] Rabbi Abraham Witty, *Exploring Jewish Tradition*, Doubleday, New York, 2001 p. 27

Endnotes

[1] T.S. Eliot, *The Sacred Wood:Essays on Poetry and Criticism* (Methune, London, 1920

[2] Alfred Edersheim, *The Temple, Its Ministry and Services* (Montville: Hendrickson Publishers, 1994) p. 37.

[3] Irwin P. Goodenough, *Jewish Symbols in the Graeco Roman Period*, Princeton University Press, Princeton, 1953 p. 28

[4] Isaiah 1:18, Leviticus 16:20-26

[5] *Hastings Dictionary of the Bible*, Hendrickson Publishers Inc., 2003

[6] *Against Heresies*, Volume 1, p. 351-352

[7] Rabbi Joseph Telushkin, *Biblical Literacy*, William Morrow and company, New York, 1997 p. 551

[8] Rabbi Abraham Witty, *Exploring Jewish Tradition*, Doubleday, New York, 2001 p. 52

[9] Ismar Elbogen, *Jewish Liturgy, A Comprehensive History*, trans. Raymond Scheindlin (Philadelphia: The Jewish Publication Society, 1993) p. 190.

[10] Rabbi Joseph Telushkin, *Jewish Literacy*, William Morrow and company, New York, 1991 p. 651

[11] Jonathan Sacks, *A Letter in the Scroll* (New York:

The Free Press, 2000) p. 39.

[12] Kevin Harris, *The Wit and Wisdom of Albert Einstein*, web site 1995

[13] Irving M. Zeitlin, *Ancient Judaism*, Polity Press, Oxford, 1984 p. 23

[14] Rabbi Joseph Telushkin, *Jewish Literacy*, William Morrow and Company, New York, 1991 p. 564-570

[15] Rabbi Joseph Telushkin, *Jewish Literacy*, William Morrow and Company, New York, 1991 p. 564-570

[16] Isaac Klein, *Guide to Jewish Religious Practice* (New York: The Jewish Theological Seminary of America, 1979

[17] Yehezkel Kaufmann, *The Religion of Israel* (Chicago: The University of Chicago Press, 1960) p. 303.

[18] Kaufman, p. 64.

[19] Isaac Klein, *Guide to Jewish Religious Practice* (New York: The Jewish Theological Seminary of America, 1979 p. 191.

[20] Joseph Heineman, *Literature of the Synagogue*, (New York, Behrman House Inc., 1975) p. 303,

[21] William Barclay, *The Revelation of John Volume 1*, Westminster Press, Philadelphia, 1976

[22] Rabbi Abraham Witty, *Exploring Jewish Tradition*, Doubleday, New York, 2001 p. 27

[23] Rabbi Joseph Telushkin, *Jewish Literacy*, William Morrow and Company, New York, 1991 p. 270

[24] Louis Jacobs, *A Jewish Theology*, (London: Darton, Longman and Todd, 1973) p. 293,294.

[25] Raphael Posner,Uri Kaploun, Shalom Cohen, *Jewish Liturgy*, Ketter Publishing House, Jerusalem, 1975 p. 32

[26] Rabbi Abraham Witty, *Exploring Jewish Tradition*, Doubleday, New York, 2001 p. 27

Bibliography

Edersheim, Alfred. *The Temple, Its Ministry and Services*. Montville: Hendrickson Publishers, 1994.

Elbogen, Ismar. *Jewish Liturgy—A Comprehensive History*. Translated by Raymond Scheindlin. Philadelphia: The Jewish Publication Society, 1993.

Heineman, Joseph. *Literature of the Synagogue*. New York: Behrman House Inc., 1975.

Jacobs, Louis. *A Jewish Theology*. London: Darton, Longman and Todd, 1973.

Kaufmann, Yehezkel. *The Religion of Israel*. Translated by Moshe Greenberg. Chicago: The University of Chicago Press, 1960.

Klein, Isaac. *Guide to Jewish Religious Practice*. New York: The Jewish Theological Seminary in America, 1979.

Sacks, Jonathan. *A Letter in the Scroll*. New York: The Free Press, 2000.

Bibliography

Edersheim, Alfred. *The Temple, Its Ministry and Services*. Montville: Hendrickson Publishers, 1994.

Elbogen, Ismar. *Jewish Liturgy—A Comprehensive History*. Translated by Raymond Scheindlin. Philadelphia: The Jewish Publication Society, 1993.

Heineman, Joseph. *Literature of the Synagogue*. New York: Behrman House Inc., 1975.

Jacobs, Louis. *A Jewish Theology*. London: Darton, Longman and Todd, 1973.

Kaufmann, Yehezkel. *The Religion of Israel*. Translated by Moshe Greenberg. Chicago: The University of Chicago Press, 1960.

Klein, Isaac. *Guide to Jewish Religious Practice*. New York: The Jewish Theological Seminary in America, 1979.

Sacks, Jonathan. *A Letter in the Scroll*. New York: The Free Press, 2000.